Battlegrou...

The Franco-Pru...
1870–1871

Battleground Series

Battleground

The Franco-Prussian War 1870–1871

Touring the Sedan Campaign

Maarten Otte

Series Editor
Nigel Cave

Pen & Sword
MILITARY

First published in Great Britain in 2020 by
Pen & Sword Military
an imprint of
Pen & Sword Books Ltd, 47 Church Street
Barnsley, South Yorkshire, S70 2AS

ISBN 978 152674 412 8

Typeset in Times New Roman by Chic Graphics

Printed and bound in England by
CPI Group (UK), Croydon, CR0 4YY

Pen & Sword Books Ltd incorporates the imprints of
Pen & Sword Archaeology, Atlas, Aviation, Battleground, Discovery,
Family History, History, Maritime, Military, Naval, Politics,
Railways, Select, Social History, Transport, True Crime,
Claymore Press, Frontline Books, Leo Cooper, Praetorian Press,
Remember When, Seaforth Publishing and Wharncliffe.

For a complete list of Pen & Sword titles please contact
PEN & SWORD BOOKS LIMITED
47 Church Street, Barnsley, South Yorkshire, S70 2AS, England
E-mail: enquiries@pen-and-sword.co.uk
Website: www.pen-and-sword.co.uk

Contents

Dedication

Dedicated to the thousands of French and German soldiers who have no known grave; and to the work of the staff of the La Dernière Cartouche Museum in Bazeilles, who keep alive the memory.

*   *   *

Soldiers from another war: Bavarian troops pose in front of a German 1870 memorial, 1915.

Series Editor's Introduction for Sedan

This is *Battleground Europe's* first venture into the Franco-Prussian War (often called on the continent the Franco-German war – geographically, at least, more accurate) and is a most welcome extension of the series into a war that was one of two that dominated the study of past campaigns (along with the American Civil War) in staff colleges or their equivalent in armies around the world from 1871. Indeed, it was a common rite of passage for ambitious officers in the major European armies to make personal tours of the major battlefields of the campaign, obviously an easier exercise than trying to range over the battlefields in the United States.

The war was one of a series that disrupted Europe in the third quarter of the nineteenth century, with vicious, generally short, campaigns involving Prussia and the German states, Denmark, Austria, France and various of the Italian states. The numerous conflicts in the Balkans in the early years of the twentieth century were considerably less significant in their impact on military thinking and the Russo-Japanese and South African wars at the turn of the century were both distant and had idiosyncrasies that made the drawing of lessons from them problematic.

It is a not uncommon allegation that the generals were unprepared, some would say culpably unprepared, for the revolutionary changes in warfare in 1914 and were cocooned in outdated certainties. That generalisation is far too sweeping and misunderstands the limitations imposed upon general staffs when they planned for war. Above all they were (and indeed are) dependent on budgets and governments and the military advisors to the latter had to prioritise expenditure. They had to face the immediate threats for which the armed forces had to be prepared and, quite rightly, this was something that was determined, in the main, by politicians and certainly by national political realities. For example, the British priority was the Royal Navy; the role of the army was as a colonial gendarmerie and certainly did not envisage, except as a remote possibility, engagement in a major European land war.

That being said, it is important to understand the impact of the Franco-Prussian War on the subsequent generations of officers, especially when it is considered that many senior commanders who took part in the First World War, especially in its first years, would have been professionally brought up under its influence. There was a huge corpus of both narrative and analytical studies that was published in the first couple of decades after the war. There was no conflict in the European theatre between its end and 1914 (excluding the geopolitical complexities of the Balkans); only the Russo-Japanese War of 1904–05 could be remotely compared to it, both in strategic importance and in the relative size and sophistication of the armed forces that were involved.

After the First World War the study of the campaigns and the short wars of the late nineteenth century by the military fell completely out of fashion; and many students today of the Great War have only a passing knowledge of the Franco-Prussian War. Yet it had a major impact on the thinking of the generals in 1914 (not to mention its influence on the politicians) – after all, it was a war from which much of the military technology dated, albeit in improved forms, in 1914. It left the legacy of a short, sharp and, above all, successful, 'war of annihilation'. The events of those first, bloody and ultimately indecisive months of fighting in 1914 determined the course of the next three years of the Great War. It follows, therefore, that a serious study of the First World War requires a basic understanding of the conduct of the War of 1870–1871. This book acts as a guide, above all, to one aspect of that war – how the cataclysmic events leading to Sedan and the end of the Third Empire developed and the significance of the ground in its outcome. At the same time the inclusion of the surviving memorials, unit and personal, made possible by Maarten Otte's extensive knowledge of the Sedan battlefields, serve to bring home the human cost of that war: it might have been short but it was very bloody.

Nigel Cave
Beaumont Hamel, March 2020

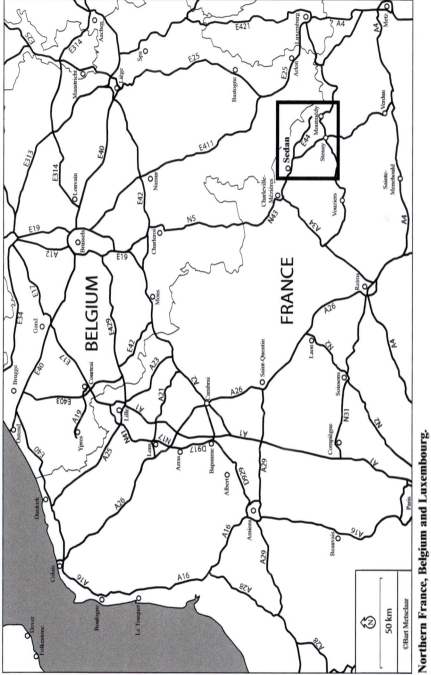

Northern France, Belgium and Luxembourg.

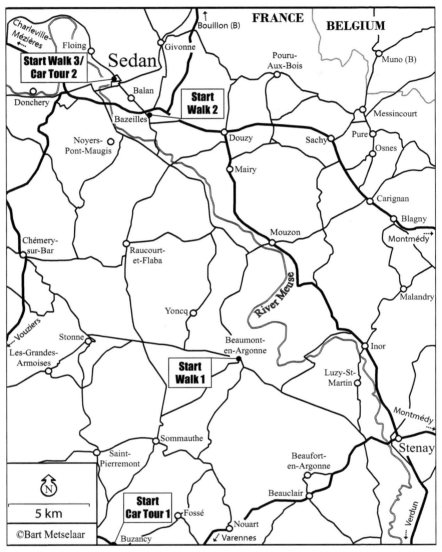

Starting points of the car tours and walks.

Introduction

As the 150th anniversary of the Franco-Prussian War is almost upon us, many people are blissfully unaware of the role this war played in shaping modern European history. While volume after volume has been published about the First and Second World Wars, the War of 1870-71 now remains largely forgotten.

On 17 July 1870, France, rather too easily provoked by the political games of the Prussians and by its own warmongering citizens, started a war that was cleverly used by the Prime Minister of Prussia and Chancellor Otto von Bismarck (1815-1898) as a means to unite the German states. The outcome of this war would indeed lead to the unification of Germany, which was to have a great effect on the European balance of power in the immediate future. Some of the seeds that would lead to the disaster of the First World War and consequently to the Second

Otto von Bismarck, 1815-1898.

World War and the Cold War, were planted during this seemingly purely local quarrel between two neighbouring countries.

For centuries, the border regions between the River Rhine and the River Meuse had been hotly disputed and had 'changed hands' several times; many people in the border area spoke both German and French. The city of Metz, for example, only became a part of France in 1648, confirmed by the Treaty of Westphalia. Yet France and Germany only became sworn enemies after the Franco-Prussian War and the unification of Germany from what had been until then a group of disparate kingdoms and principalities.

In 1870, although not yet united, the states of Germany under Prussian leadership managed to defeat two French armies within a month; this was a great coup for the Germans as France was the leading continental European power at the time and arguably, on paper, the greatest military power; however, Prussia was an expanding kingdom and had recently fought and won wars against Denmark (1864) and the Austrian Empire (1866) and had a large, well equipped and fine army. Although most of the French Army, the Emperor including, had surrendered after such a brief campaign, perhaps bizarrely, Paris and the new Government did not, proclaiming the Third Republic. A siege of Paris ensued but finally, after several months of fighting, famine and the shelling of Paris, on 26 January 1871 an armistice was signed.

The German victory parade in Paris, 1871.

Sedan Day, Brandenburg Gate, Berlin, 2 September 1871.

The disaster of Sedan and the bitter humiliation imposed on the French by the Germans when they declared Wilhelm I, King of Prussia, Emperor of a united Germany in the Hall of Mirrors in Versailles (1871), were more than enough to stoke the fire of hatred against the Germans. After the devastating defeat of the French on 1 September 1870 at Sedan, generations of Germans celebrated 'Sedan Day' on 2 September, the day of the capitulation. Nationalism became deeply rooted in both French and German societies, which hampered the development of mutual understanding between the neighbours.

King Wilhelm I of Prussia, 1797-1888.

The German annexation of the prosperous provinces of Alsace and Lorraine in 1871, particularly their coal mines and iron ore deposits, to ensure payment of war reparations and to function as a buffer zone, was almost a certain guarantee of a future war between Germany and France and certainly poisoned relations between them. The unified Germany that emerged from the ashes of the Franco-Prussian War was a powerful, self-confident, central power. The earlier defeat of Austria-Hungary, now followed by the defeat of the French and with Britain adopting a policy of 'splendid isolation', focussed on her colonies, paved the way for German dominance of Europe.

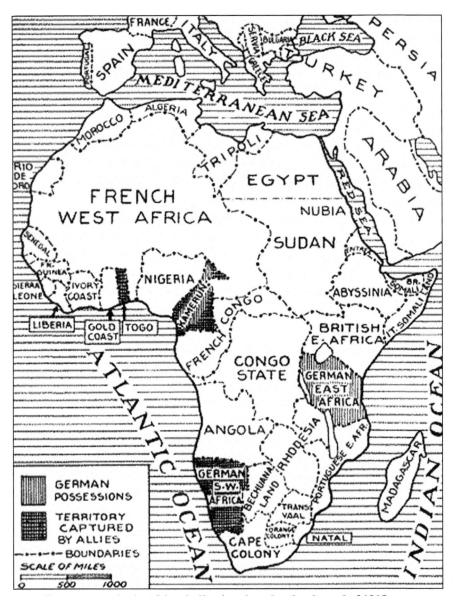

German colonies in Africa, indicating those lost by the end of 1915.

Many Germans in the late nineteenth century viewed colonial acquisitions as a true indication of having achieved nationhood and developed international prestige, so Germany became involved in the Scramble for Africa. With the Germans joining the race for the last uncharted territories that had not yet been carved up, competition for colonies involved all major European nations and several lesser powers, like Belgium. From 1884, under Chancellor Otto von Bismarck, who was initially not very keen on the idea, the Germans seized German East Africa (present-day Tanzania [minus Zanzibar], Rwanda and Burundi), and German South-West Africa, present-day Namibia and a part of Botswana. Modern Cameroon, Togo and a small part of Ghana also belonged to their African Schutzgebiete, or protectorates, as well as several islands in the Pacific (The Bismarck Archipelago). These prestigious African and Pacific colonies, at least to German eyes, went hand-in-hand with dreams of a High Seas Fleet. Germany's colonial aspirations were initially not taken too seriously by the other European powers – Italy had also entered a crowded field when she too was unified in 1870. However, with the establishment of the High Seas Fleet (which concerned the British particularly and was of major concern by the turn of the century), economic and industrial prosperity, with colonial 'pretensions' and an eagerness to rise to the status of superpower, many countries in Europe began to view Germany with suspicion and concern. This suspicion led to several mutual assistance treaties which, in turn, would become one of the reasons for the outbreak of the First World War and its rapid spread amongst European nations.

After my first visit to the former battlefields of the Franco-Prussian War, many years ago now, I was rather surprised to discover how little modern-day literature is available on the subject. However, during my quest for literature and maps, I found out that before 1914 the 1870-1871 Franco-German conflict was by far the most studied war by the general staffs of the major world armies. As a result, in the period 1871-1914 many hundreds of books were written on the subject. The machine gun, breech-loading guns and rifles, telegraph, railroads, the development of shells were all examined: without doubt, the application of these new inventions turned this conflict into the first 'modern' European war. No wonder the generals and the students in military academies studied the Franco-Prussian War so closely (along with the American Civil War) so that they could apply these new technologies in any future war. It was the last major war fought in Europe, outside the Balkans, before 1914; and, naturally, it was completely overshadowed by that conflict.

In France, the 1870-1871 war is largely forgotten although many of the French are interested in the era of the Second Empire, from about 1850-1870; there is even a bi-monthly magazine devoted to it. However, as regards military conflicts, in France the main focus lies with the First and Second World Wars. Having said that it is also fair to say that today the Germans show possibly even less interest in the 1870-1871 war.

The Germans made it difficult for the French to forget about the humiliation of defeat, not least because of the payment of huge reparations and the annexation of Alsace-Lorraine. According to the Treaty of Frankfurt (10 May 1871), the Germans insisted on erecting monuments on French soil to commemorate their fallen comrades. By and large, most of the 1870 monuments in the Sedan area are of German make. On 4 April 1873, a law was enacted in France that field graves, French and German, should be respected: some remained where they were; others were exhumed and reburied in mass graves. The collection of bodies took place mainly between 1876 and 1880. The necessary land concessions, almost invariably in existing communal cemeteries, were bought by the French government. Because of this, mass graves and individual monuments

The original Treaty of Frankfurt. (Otto von Bismarck Archive, Friedrichsruh)

that are spread across the battlefield are protected in perpetuity. Originally, each 1870 monument was fenced off by a green wrought iron fence bearing the inscription *Tombes militaires, loi du 4 avril 1873*. Unfortunately, most of the original fences have since disappeared.

Today, many of the monuments are derelict, as almost no maintenance has been carried out for a very long time. Great credit must be given to the Souvenir Français organization, which since 1906 has restored many of the individual (including many German) grave monuments that were built in small cemeteries in hamlets and villages scattered around Sedan. To the people living in these areas, especially between 1870 and 1914, these monuments have been a permanent reminder of the French defeat. Today, the events of 1870 are largely obscured by the two world wars of the twentieth century.

After many visits I decided that this fascinating but largely forgotten battlefield and the tens of thousands of soldiers who lost their lives here deserved a better fate. After explaining the importance of this war to other people time and again I decided that the time had come to share my findings in a book. The historical research for the first chapter, *France and Germany 1860-1870*, has been done by my friend and battlefield companion Bart, with whom I explored most of the area; the excellent maps included in the tour section were drawn by him.

A note of clarification: in this book I apply the term 'German army' to the Prussian-led collective armies of the German states. The Prussian army was the biggest and most powerful but there were also armies from Bavaria, Saxony etc. At the end of the Franco-Prussian War in 1871 and following the unification of Germany, the German army came into being. From 1871-1918, the period of the German Empire until the abolition of the monarchies after the Armistice at the end of WWI, there was an

Emblem of the *Souvenir Français.*

Imperial German Navy but not a centrally commanded Imperial German Army, as a number of states retained a certain element of 'independence', which also extended to their armies; these armies collectively were simply described as the German Army.

The narrative is brief but I hope sufficient for a basic understanding of the chronology of events – for those who wish to know more, there are some suggestions in the bibliography and further reading section at the end of this book. Consequently much has been omitted that distract from the main story; it is not the aim of this book to deliver a complete and definitive history of the Sedan Campaign 1870; *au contraire*, it is to encourage you to get you out of your chairs – or perhaps divert from a holiday destination for a day or two – and visit the battlefield yourselves.

The monuments and grave memorials that have survived today are situated in the beautiful landscape of the French Ardennes; they stand in silent remembrance of the men who were killed here 150 years ago in a war that undoubtedly dramatically changed the course of European history. The Franco-Prussian War (and to a lesser extent the Crimean War of 1853-1856) stands as a necessary precursor to the First World War and, by extension, to the Second World War, the Iron Curtain and the Cold War. Therefore, I am very pleased that Pen & Sword Books, after some persuading, have had the courage to take the risk of publishing this book, in my opinion on an important but relatively little known campaign, in the Battleground Europe series. Personally, I think this history needs to be studied at least briefly by any student of the Great War. As usual, the tours and walks will take you to many sites of interest which, hopefully, will give you a clearer insight into the three days of heavy fighting that took place in the Sedan area. You will be following in the footsteps of literally hundreds, indeed thousands, of serving officers in professional armies throughout the world who came to examine the campaign in the forty or so years between 1871 and 1914.

List of Maps

CHAPTER 1

France and Germany, 1860-1870:
a complex geopolitical rivalry

Napoleon III, Emperor of France 1851-1870.
At the time of the election of Louis Napoleon (1808-1873) as the first (and only) President of the new Second French Republic in 1848, the French sought to become the premier power in Europe once more. With the *coup d'état* of 2 December 1851, Napoleon ended the constitution of the Second Republic and became almost absolute ruler. This was the same day and month as when his famous uncle, Napoleon I, crowned himself Emperor of France in Notre Dame Cathedral in Paris in 1804. On 2 December 1852, by means of a national referendum that voted in favour of Napoleon, the Second

Emperor Napoleon III, 1808-1873.

Republic was transformed into the Second Empire, making Napoleon III the Emperor of France.

The other European powers were not overly enthusiastic; they feared a return to the state of affairs in the Napoleonic era. Indeed, the French saw it as a new chance to play an important role in Europe and the world and finally to forget about the defeat at Waterloo in 1815. In spite of all of this, the French people remained divided; the Royalist Bourbonists were not at all happy; the restoration of the Bourbon Dynasty seemed further away than ever. What the newly installed emperor needed to unite his people was a war and, lo and behold, in the Crimea trouble was brewing; the answer to Louis Napoleon's prayers.

The Crimean War (1853-1856).
This was a war that originated in rivalry between the Russians and the Ottoman Empire, the latter going through a period of long decline.

1

The Crimea, 1853-1856.

Although intervening on the side of the Turks, the Crimean War offered Napoleon III the chance to intimidate the Turks and to prevent Russia from becoming too powerful in Europe, especially amongst the newly emerging countries arising from the crumbling Ottoman Empire. It also afforded him the opportunity of portraying himself as the protector of Latin Christianity, as opposed to the Russian championing of the Orthodox. The French even cooperated with their arch-enemies, the British, who wanted to ensure that Russia had no access to the Mediterranean Sea and thus keep any Tsarist expansionist plans firmly under control.

On 13 September 1854, the combined French and British fleet landed close to Sevastopol, in the Crimea. Initially planned as a lightning war to take the major Russian Black Sea ports, it soon became a slogging match with extensive trenches, continuous shelling, cavalry charges and huge numbers of casualties. In 1855, the Russian 'Generals', January and February, ie the Russian winter, resulted in an enormous number of casualties amongst the allies. Finally, on 12 September 1855, after a siege of eleven months, the Russians evacuated Sevastopol. Paris, Turin (the rising Kingdom of Piedmont Sardinia had also become involved) and London were ecstatic. On 25 February 1856, the peace negotiations started in Paris; France's honour had been saved; once again it had become an important player in Europe. The fact that during the conflict 100,000 Frenchmen had died, mainly of disease, malnutrition and the cold, in no particular order, was quickly discounted by the Emperor. However, thousands of families had lost their loved ones and they did not forget. Even today there are still numerous streets and farms in France that are named after Sevastopol.

2

Otto von Bismarck.

In Germany the political situation changed rapidly when in 1862 the ambitious Otto von Bismarck (1815-1898) became Minister President of the kingdom of Prussia. He wanted to forge all the disparate German states into a united Germany. Prussia's victory in the war against the Danes over Schleswig-Holstein in 1864 was an excellent indicator with which to impress the south German states, traditionally dominated by Austria. However, the Catholic Kingdom of Bavaria refused to join Protestant Prussia and chose to side with the Austrian Empire when Prussia declared war on Austria in 1866. When the outcome of that war went in favour of Prussia, the Bavarian King Ludwig II had to bow his head to the wishes of the now very powerful King Wilhelm of Prussia. In 1867 Bismarck became Chancellor of the North German Confederation. In the same year Austria was transformed into a Dual Monarchy, Austria-Hungary, with its focus away from Germany and towards the Balkans. After the military victories of 1864 and 1866, and the other major German power safely out of the way, the architect of German unity needed a further war to convince the rest of the German states, particularly those of the south, of his plan.

Otto von Bismarck, 1815-1898.

King Ludwig II of Bavaria (popularly known as 'Mad King Ludwig'), 1845-1886.

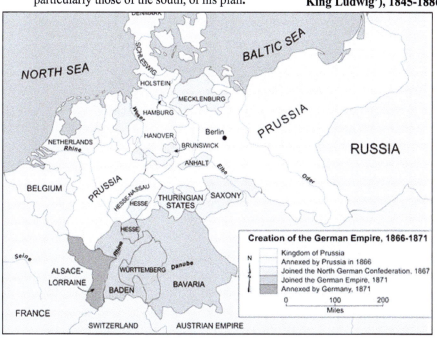

The expansion of what became the German Empire.

The Luxembourg Crisis.

Bismarck almost got his way quicker than he anticipated during the spring of 1867, when a diplomatic dispute between the Second Empire and the Germans almost led to war. In 1866 secret negotiations were held between Prussia and France not to meddle in each other's territorial gains and, effectively, in their respective spheres of influence. Soon thereafter, Bismarck set his eyes on the province of Limburg in the Netherlands, east of the River Meuse. Eventually it was agreed that Limburg would remain part of the Dutch Kingdom under King William III, on the condition that the area would be incorporated into the North German Confederation.

France, on the other hand, turned its attention on the Great Duchy of Luxembourg, which was part of a personal union with the Netherlands. To prevent France from invading Luxembourg, King William III tried to place the Grand Duchy in the North German Confederation. Bismarck refused this proposal on account of the secret negotiations between France and Germany.

As a result of Bismarck's refusal, on 23 March 1867 William III permitted the sale of Luxembourg to France on the condition that Prussia agreed to the deal. The news of the French deal was quickly picked up by the press of the countries involved and caused outrage. The

The reduction of Luxembourg, 1659 -1870.

newspapers in Prussia were full of indignation at the bargain sale of Luxembourg; was it not the House of Luxembourg that provided four emperors to the former Holy Empire, and therefore was a significant part in German history? Many argued that Germany needed Luxembourg as a buffer between her and France.

The diplomatic crisis resulted in the partial mobilisation of both Prussia and France, fuelled by demonstrations in Luxembourg by supporters of France, Prussia and the Netherlands. The latter group of protesters demonstrated under the motto: 'Mir wëlle bleiwe wat mir sin' (We want to stay what we are), which remains the motto of Luxembourg. A startled France quickly broke off the negotiations with the Dutch king to avoid a war. Bismarck was relieved, for he knew very well that Prussia and her allies within Germany were not yet ready for a war with France.

Under Russian auspices and with the agreement of the British, who were anxious to keep both major powers out of Luxembourg, the Congress of London was held in May 1867, where it was agreed that: France would renounce her claims to the Grand Duchy of Luxembourg and that William III, King of the Netherlands, remained ruler of Luxembourg as Grand Duke; Prussia removed its garrison from the capital, Luxembourg City; the neutrality of Luxembourg was guaranteed by the signatories of the Congress; and that Dutch Limburg and the Grand Duchy of Luxembourg remained in the North German [Economic] Union, the *Zollverein*.

The French army in 1870.
During the Crimean War the French troops were a superior fighting force to their British counterparts. In terms of size, supplies, weaponry and guns the British generals could only look on in awe. Since the Napoleonic Wars the British army had been, effectively, a colonial gendarmerie, tasked with maintaining order in the Empire. What expenditure there was on the forces tended to be concentrated, understandably, on the Royal Navy.

Under Napoleon III the French army continued to expand and develop rapidly. Thus, by 1870, Waterloo was but a distant memory for the French and since their success in the Crimea they had become ever more confident in their military capabilities. Indeed, the French developed and introduced the cartridge-fed rifle, which replaced the now obsolete front-loading guns; whilst the French army was the first to provide serious amounts of reliable small arms firepower in their ranks in the form of machine guns, *mitrailleuses*.

However, in contrast, by 1870 the army's battle tactics had become hopelessly outdated – lessons that might usefully have been learnt from the American Civil War of 1861-65, which resulted in up to a million

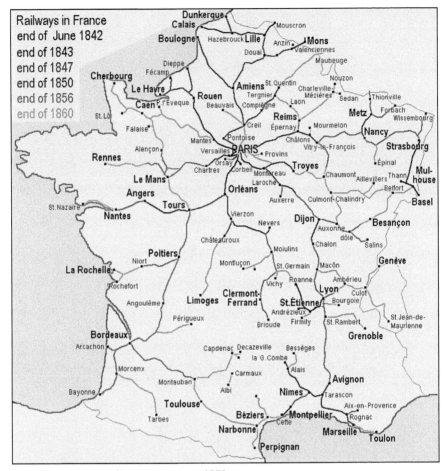

The French railway system ca. 1870.

casualties, military and civilian, were not absorbed. The mobilization plan was fundamentally flawed, bedevilled by a catalogue of bad logistics, in spite of the modern railway network that had by this stage been built across the whole of France. The French would very quickly find out that fighting a modern European army was a world away from fighting a colonial war in Africa.

The Reffye machine gun.

Napoleon III was very interested in the development of the machine gun. Montigny, a Belgian inventor who had built a hand-cranked machine gun, approached the French Army to sell them the new weapon. Experiments to evaluate the weapon began in 1863 in a French test facility near Paris, but the decision was made to build a similar weapon using French parts

6

only. The manufacture of such a weapon began at Meudon in 1866, under the direction of Verchères de Reffye (1821-1880) and with the secret help of Montigny. Hence, the weapon is usually referred to as the Reffye machine gun, model 1866.

Before the outbreak of the Franco-Prussian War, 215 machine guns had been manufactured for the French army. They were of the 13mm (a slightly larger calibre than .50), twenty-five-barrel type, and used elongated shotgun shell style cartridges. The weapon, which was mounted on an artillery carriage, was deployed in six-gun batteries and manned by artillery personnel. As a consequence of making it a part of the artillery rather than the infantry, most of the time they were used quite ineffectively to engage distant targets, being treated as an artillery piece.

The Reyffe machine gun.

By coincidence the weapon was used during the Battle of Gravelotte in the infantry support role and at shorter distances. It produced devastating effects and it gained the respect of the German soldiers. Around 150–250 shots per minute could be fired, depending on the skills of the operator; changing magazines was not an easy task, especially when the gun heated up. The whole weapon was very cumbersome, weighing around 910 kilos, some 2,000 pounds. Although the tactical use of this weapon was still in its infancy, the Germans on the receiving end were very impressed by the French machine guns. They quickly understood its potential for future wars; at the start of the First World War, the German army was equipped with an estimated 12,000 machine guns, significantly more than any other country could muster at that time.

The Krupp breech loading gun.

A rifled breech loader is an artillery piece which, unlike the smooth-bore cannon and rifled muzzle loader that preceded it, has rifling (the helical groove pattern that is machined into the internal surface of the barrel of a gun) and is loaded from the breech at the rear of the gun; it was a revolutionary new invention. The spin imparted by the gun's rifling gave projectiles directional stability and increased range. Loading from the rear of the gun left the crew less exposed to enemy fire, allowed smaller gun emplacements or turrets and a faster rate of fire. The German company Krupp adopted horizontal sliding block breeches for all artillery calibres up to 16 inch (40 cm.) naval guns.

The shell and powder cartridge were inserted through the open rear end of the breech into the gun bore; a steel block was slid home into a horizontal slot cut through the breech to close the rear end of the breech. This system allowed a much higher rate of fire and also made it safer for the gun crew to handle their piece. There was no need for separate gun powder charges any more, as the propellant for the shell was now (relatively) safely packed away in a shell casing, much like an ordinary rifle cartridge. The work horse for the German Armies was the Krupp 87mm M1866 field gun. The rate of fire, the accuracy and the number of

A Krupp breech loading gun, 1866.

Krupp guns deployed by the Germans played a pivotal role during the Franco-German War. With the Krupp gun, mechanized slaughter was introduced to the battlefield. More French troops were killed or mutilated by exploding shells than by rifle fire.

From the Spanish Succession Crisis of 1868, to the French declaration of war on Germany.

In 1868, the case of the Spanish Succession heightened tensions between France and Prussia. On 30 September 1868, Queen Isabella II of Spain, who had been accused of intrigue and interfering with the government, was deposed in the Glorious Revolution; she went into exile in France. After a string of failed attempts to fill the vacancy on the throne, the south German and Catholic Hohenzollern, Prince Leopold, a relative of King Wilhelm I of Prussia, was put forward as a successor to the throne, strongly supported by Bismarck. However, France feared the extension of Prussian influence and encirclement and would not allow a Hohenzollern to sit on the Spanish throne. For Prussia it was important to put Leopold on to the Spanish throne; not only would it gain them prestige but there was also the added benefit of having a strong ally on France's southern borders.

Isabella II of Spain, 1830-1904.

Prince Leopold of Hohenzollern, 1835-1905.

Other possible candidates for the throne were rejected by the Spanish and so, in February 1870, Leopold became a strong contender once again. This time, Bismarck, strongly supported by Moltke (Chief of Staff of the Prussian Army) and Roon (Minister of War), was more vigorous in his bid to secure the Spanish throne. On the other hand, both King Wilhelm I (1861-1888) and the intended successor, Leopold, were

The Prussian Chief of Staff, von Moltke the Elder (from 1871 Chief of the Great General Staff), 1800-1891.

Albrecht von Roon, Prussian Minister of War, 1803-1879.

reluctant – they considered that the situation in Spain was too unstable and that it might stir anti-Prussian sentiments throughout Europe. Bismarck managed to convince Leopold's father, Prince Karl Anton, of his obligations in the situation. Leopold reluctantly agreed. King Wilhelm, who had been kept in the dark during these developments, was annoyed by the whole affair but had no choice but to give his support 'with a very heavy heart' to the candidacy.

Herzog von Gramont.

French Minister of Foreign Affairs, the Duke de Gramont, 1819-1880.

French politicians on both sides of the political spectrum were not satisfied and demanded further guarantees from the Prussians. The more headstrong and, generally, conservative amongst them sought war with Prussia to have French prestige restored and, more important, to bring the Ollivier administration down – a government that had managed to turn the Empire into a constitutional monarchy as recently as April 1870.

During July 1870 events escalated quickly, largely due to the media fuelling popular opinion to the brink of hysteria. In Paris, the newspapers demanded that France should not give into Prussian demands on the question of the Spanish throne. The Prussian Government, however, refused to acknowledge the situation, as the intrigue was officially non-existent. Tensions were further increased by the French Minister of Foreign Affairs Gramont and Prime Minister Émile Ollivier, the latter in particular a staunch advocate of the French cause and reluctant to follow a diplomatic solution. A stirring speech by Gramont to the French Parliament on 6 July could be interpreted as an ultimatum. The speech was drafted

French Prime Minister Ollivier, 1825-1913.

by Gramont, the final paragraph was written by Ollivier and with the approval of Napoleon III – by this stage a sick man and whose political powers had been significantly curtailed since the start of his reign. The French demanded that this candidate be withdrawn and that the Prussians promise not to renew their candidacy to the Spanish throne – if the Prussians failed to comply with their demands, then there would be war.

Leopold's candidacy was withdrawn on 12 July. But for the French this was not good enough. They wanted assurances from the Prussians that there would be no more Prussian candidates for the Spanish throne. This message was courteously delivered to King Wilhelm at his summer residence in Ems, a spa town in Hesse-Nassau, a province of the Kingdom of Prussia, by Count Vincent Benedetti, the French ambassador. A disturbed Wilhelm declined to give any such assurances.

The next day, on 13 July, a telegram was sent from Ems to Bismarck in Berlin by Heinrich Abeken, officially the Privy Councillor of Legation in the Prussian Ministry of Foreign Affairs but in fact amongst the most important political figures in Prussia. The telegram contained a report of the meeting between Wilhelm and Benedetti. The original text of what became known as the Ems Telegram reads:

'Ems, July 13, 1870. To the Federal Chancellor Count Bismarck, No. 61, 3:10 p.m. Station Ems. (RUSH)

His Majesty the King [Wilhelm I] writes to me: 'M. Benedetti intercepted me on the Promenade in order to demand of me most insistently that I should authorize him to telegraph immediately to Paris that I shall obligate myself for all future

French diplomat Count Benedetti, 1817-1900.

time never again to give my approval to the candidacy of the Hohenzollerns should it be renewed. I refused to agree to this, the last time somewhat severely, informing him that one dare not and cannot assume such obligations *à tout jamais*. Naturally, I informed him that I had received no news as yet, and since he had been informed earlier than I, by way of Paris and Madrid, he could easily understand that my Government was once again out of the matter. Since then His Majesty has received a dispatch from the Prince [Karl Anton]. As His Majesty informed Count Benedetti that he was expecting news from the Prince, His Majesty himself, in view of the above-mentioned demand and in consonance with the advice of Count Eulenburg and myself, decided not to receive the French envoy again but to inform him through an adjutant that His Majesty had now received from the Prince confirmation of the news which

Benedetti had already received from Paris, and that he had nothing further to say to the Ambassador. His Majesty leaves it to the judgment of Your Excellency whether or not to communicate at once the new demand by Benedetti and its rejection to our ambassadors and to the press.'

The original 'Emscher Depèche' – 'The Ems Telegram'.

Bismarck was already very annoyed at France's humiliating demands of the previous days. Now that he had this telegram he saw an opportunity and seized it with both hands. Before sending the telegram to Prussian envoys in the other German states and releasing it to the newspapers and public, Bismarck edited the text of the original telegram to make it look as if Wilhelm had been insulted by the French Ambassador; the telegram had been shortened in such a way that it would also give the French the impression that their ambassador had been snubbed by the king.

'After the reports of the renunciation by the hereditary Prince of Hohenzollern had been officially transmitted by the Royal Government of Spain to the Imperial Government of France, the French Ambassador presented to His Majesty the King at Ems the demand to authorize him to telegraph to Paris that His Majesty the King would obligate himself for all future time never again to give his approval to the candidacy of the Hohenzollerns should it be renewed. His Majesty the King thereupon refused to receive the French envoy again and informed him through an adjutant that His Majesty has nothing further to say to the Ambassador.'

Bismarck's editing had the desired results in Paris; Empress Eugénie, a staunch advocate of war (to emphasize France's power and prestige in Europe and to protect the Bonaparte dynasty), encouraged anti-Prussian sentiments in Paris, which by now had reached fever pitch.

The outbreak of war.

The decision to call up the reserves of the French Army was taken on the afternoon of 14 July, Bastille Day; on 15 July the French Parliament and Senate voted overwhelmingly in favour of war. When news of the French decision reached the German authorities, Bismarck and Moltke gave the order for mobilisation of the

The Empress Eugénie (de Montijo), 1826-1920.

Prussian Army. Bismarck had cleverly manoeuvred France into the role of aggressor in this conflict so that the southern German States would also side with Prussia and the North German Confederation. France formally declared war on Prussia on 17 July, the declaration arriving in Berlin on the 19th whilst the North German Reichstag – established in 1867 – was in session.

Mobilization.

The Germans mobilized their armies according to prearranged plans and prepared their troops for transport to the Franco-Prussian border. Reservists were called to their district depots, where they were armed and equipped and sent to the nearest station; meanwhile, many men volunteered for the army; they also had to be administered. The German mobilisation operation was better planned – after all, many of the German states had had recent experience of the process in 1864 and 1866. The French had huge problems organizing transport, equipment and rations for their reservists; however, their regular army was organized and deployed mostly according to plan.

Prince Friedrich Karl of Hohenzollern, 1828-1885.

By 1 August, a fortnight after the French declaration of war, the Germans had managed to muster almost 400,000 men, over 150,000 horses and 1,200 guns, organized into three Armies, on a 150 kilometres length of front roughly along the border, from Luxembourg in the north to Wissembourg in the south. The First Army was commanded by General von Steinmetz, 60,000 men; the Second by Prince Friedrich Karl (nephew of Wilhelm and an experienced, competent commander and military theorist), 194,000 men; and the Third, commanded by Crown Prince [of Prussia] Friedrich, 130,000 men

The Germans had anticipated that the French would mobilize faster than they could. Helmuth von Moltke, the almost seventy years old Chief of the Prussian General Staff, feared a French invasion before the German armies were battle ready, a fundamental concern that did not transpire. Although the French started mobilizing their troops as early as 6 July, three weeks later

King Wilhelm I of Prussia, 1797-1888.

there were only 250,000 men on her eastern border. Despite numerous logistical planning issues (for example, rifles were sent to the front without ammunition), the French railway system operated at least adequately: an estimated fifty-five trains managed to reach the front each day.

On Tuesday 26 July, British journalist Edward Legge, who travelled in the wake of the German army from Cologne to Sedan, reported:

> 'I found Cologne Station thronged with soldiers and the good townsfolk suffering from a sharp attack of war fever. They apprehended onslaught upon their city. The French were at Forbach and there was a rumour that they intended to march to Cologne, or sail down the Rhine in their gunboats! Preparations were at once made to defend the town. The fortifications were inspected and ordered to be increased; the lumbering old cannon were cleaned and generally furbished up [refurbished]; the trees around the city walls were all cut down, so that they might not interfere with the cannon fire when the enemy should arrive and it was even feared that the beautiful public gardens would have to be despoiled and the charming country houses in the suburbs destroyed, on account of the hindrance which they would offer to the cannonade from inside the walls.
>
> Nothing but war was talked about. In a very practical way the inhabitants set about their self-imposed task of assisting the soldiers and providing them with provisions and cigars. Every train brought in thousands of spike-helmeted, blue-tunicked men, all ahungered and athirst after their long journey. Ladies and gentlemen – professional men and shopkeepers – all who had a few thalers to bestow upon the defenders of the Fatherland – waited the arrival of the soldier-trains; waited with their baskets choking with *butter-brod* [bread], *käse* [cheese], *schinken* [ham], red wine and cigars and when the trains came in it was marvellous how quickly all these good things were disposed of. They have tremendous appetites, the German *soldaten*, and their capacity for drinking is illimitable.'

The command structure of the French army was not clear and central planning was virtually non-existent. Ironically, the biggest problem facing the French High Command was Emperor Napoleon III himself, who at the very last moment decided to take personal command of the army. ('A Bonaparte belongs at the head of his army!') The carefully prepared plans of General Lebœuf, dating from 1868, were discarded and during mobilisation a new plan had to be hastily drawn up. This and the elimination of the French High Command were a guaranteed recipe of disaster – and a precious gift to the Germans.

On 28 July the Emperor, suffering from a chronic bladder stone, left for Metz. Arriving late in the afternoon, he took up residence at the Prefecture, while army headquarters were set up at the Hôtel de L'Europe. Upon Napoleon's arrival he assumed command of the newly titled Army of the Rhine. Escorted by a large household, Napoleon also brought with him his fourteen year old son, the Prince Imperial, Eugène Louis Napoleon Bonaparte. Before leaving Paris, Napoleon had made Empress Eugénie regent in his absence.

Marshal Bazaine, 1811-1888.

That evening at the Hôtel de L'Europe, the new army commander asked his generals and marshals for suggestions as how to conduct a campaign against Prussia, a bad omen of things to come. After Marshal Bazaine's answer that he had nothing to suggest (Bazaine was the field commander of III Corps), it became painfully obvious that there was in fact no real plan besides waiting for the Germans to make the first move. Smoking one cigarette after another and suffering badly from a bladder stone, Napoleon was under massive pressure to launch a major attack.

While the Germans were massing on France's borders, more bad news from his generals in the field arrived at Napoleon's headquarters in the form of letters and telegrams. It appeared that many of the French divisions were thousands of men short, reserves were still on their way to the front. There was a shortage of almost everything, especially coffee, sugar, rice, salt, water and, above all, bread. Adding to these problems, most of the newly arrived troops at the border region were armed with the new Chassepot rifle but there was almost no ammunition available. The troops also showed little discipline and motivation and were stretched out over 250 kilometres, outnumbered by the Germans three to two.

From north to south the French troops, each corps consisting of four divisions, were deployed as follows:

16

Troops stationed in the area around Metz:

    IV Corps, commanded by General Ladmirault
    II Corps, commanded by General Frossard
    III Corps, commanded by Marshal Bazaine
    The Imperial Guard, commanded by General Bourbaki

Troops deployed south east of Metz, to defend the French border from north of Strasbourg to the Swiss border in the south:

    V Corps, commanded by General de Failly
    I Corps, commanded by Marshal MacMahon
    VII Corps, commanded by General Douay

VI Corps, commanded by Marshal Canrobert, lay in reserve at Châlons Camp, Châlons-sur-Marne.

CHAPTER 2

From Saarbrücken to Metz,
2-18 August

First blood, Tuesday 2 August, the skirmish at Saarbrücken.

Fortunately for Napoleon, who had only very limited military experience, on 27 July General Frossard came up with a plan to launch a small-scale attack at the border town of Saarbrücken to test the strength of the German army and to discover their whereabouts. Naturally, Napoleon quickly agreed. A few hours earlier, reconnaissance by the French cavalry had determined that only a weak Prussian garrison, commanded by Major General Gneisenau, was holding the town. Sensing an easy victory, on Sunday 31 July Napoleon ordered the army forward and some 5,000 men of Frossard's II Corps crossed the River Saar to seize Saarbrücken.

General Frossard, 1807-1875.

That same day, the journalist Edward Legge, who was staying in a hotel in St. Johann, a suburb of Saarbrücken, noted:

> 'All the soldiers were dispatched to the frontier in the south. Train after train, steamer after steamer, teaming with men, baggage and artillery, were destined for that point where it was believed the enemy would make an attack [roughly between Saarbrücken and Wissembourg]. In reply to my questions to several of them today as to what was the cause of the war they said they did not know; they were fighting for the King!'

Frossard's II Corps and Marshal Bazaine's III Corps crossed the German border on Tuesday, 2 August and began to force the Prussian 40th Regiment of the 16th Division out of the town of Saarbrücken with a series of frontal attacks. The first French shells started to explode in Bellevue, a village about a kilometre south of Saarbrücken. Edward Legge, who was out visiting a German artillery battalion that morning saw it:

'The bivouac was broken up, the artillery limbered up and the whole battalion was under arms in about a quarter of an hour. It was no time for delay, for the news brought by the orderly was that the enemy had driven in the Prussian *vorposten* [outposts]

Marshal Bazaine.

at Bellevue and had taken up positions on the heights commanding Saarbrücken. Looking towards the heights, I saw a formidable array of French soldiers and artillery planted in entrenchments which had been thrown up with great rapidity. Several Prussian detachments were soon marching across the fields towards the railway bridge near Barbach; almost simultaneously with this movement some grenades and bullets flew over our heads and all was bustle and animation. The war had begun!'

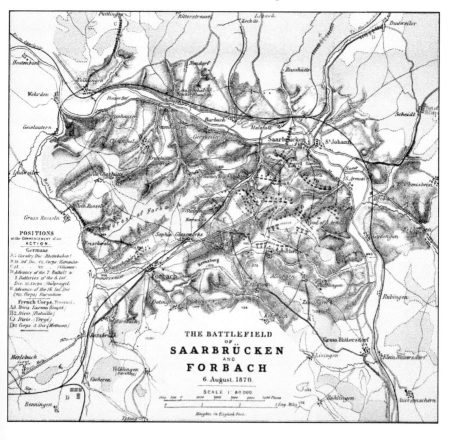

THE BATTLEFIELD
OF ..
SAARBRÜCKEN
AND
FORBACH
6 August 1870.

SCALE 1: 80.000.

Heights in English Feet.

The Chassepot rifle really proved its worth against the Dreyse rifle, as French riflemen easily outranged their German counterparts in the skirmishes around Bellevue, St. Johann and Saarbrücken. Overwhelmed by the French, who attacked in superior numbers, the Germans withdrew; exactly as they had been ordered to do in this kind of situation. In spite of this, the Prussians put up strong resistance; the French suffered eighty-six casualties to the Prussian eighty-three. Contrary to all expectations, Napoleon had beaten Moltke in making the first move and managed to secure a first, albeit small, French victory. The problem, however, was that there was no back-up plan; the French did not press home the attack; instead, after a few hours they left the town altogether. If there had been further orders to invade Germany while the Prussians were not yet fully organized, it is possible that the course of events could have been different. It was almost if the French were not really aware of the seriousness of the situation, as if they were playing a war game.

Napoleon had witnessed the fighting in the company of his son, the Prince Imperial. It was his son's first experience of war; some sources mention that he picked up a German bullet as a souvenir. The Germans, unbroken in spirit by this minor set back, made fun of the prince; they had christened him the 'Mitrailleuse Prinz', as it was reported that he fired the first burst of machine-gun fire at Saarbrücken.

The French artillery had caused considerable damage, especially in St. Johann and Bellevue. Edward Legge:

'When I arrived at the scene of the battle, what a change had come over the landscape! The road was strewn with branches of trees, bits of grenade and shrapnel, rifle bullets, pieces of uniform, a *zündnadel* or two [German type of rifle], a sword bayonet here and there. What had been verdant fields in the morning were now charred wastes. A little inn near the bivouac was in flames; along the road were dead and mangled horses; near St. Johann I found other cottages burnt down […].'

While ordinary Frenchmen hailed the invasion as the first step towards the Rhineland and fantasized about taking Berlin, General Frossard was receiving alarming reports of Prussian and Bavarian armies massing to the south east, in addition to the forces to the north and north east.

Thursday 4 August, the Battle of Wissembourg.
On learning that the German Second Army (194,000 men) was just forty-eight kilometres away and was moving towards Saarbrücken and the border in the Wissembourg area, General Frossard hastily withdrew the

Army of the Rhine in the direction of Spicheren and Forbach, which were easier to defend. Marshal MacMahon, however, unaware of German movements beyond vague rumours in the newspapers, left his four divisions of I Corps spread thirty-two kilometres apart in depth to react to any German invasion. Having to maintain contact with Bazaine to the north and Failly in the south, this resulted in a very thin line of soldiers protecting the Wissembourg sector. Oblivious of the danger, they continued to watch the Rhine crossings. Meanwhile, MacMahon ordered the 2nd Division to take up positions at Wissembourg, unaware of the fact that Moltke had ordered the German armies to start the invasion of Alsace early on the morning of Saturday 6 August at exactly that spot. The French 2nd Division was now on a collision course with the German Third Army.

Originally Moltke had aimed to surround the whole of Napoleon's army; now he first wanted to take care of the French II and V Corps in the east and later deal a second blow in the Metz sector.

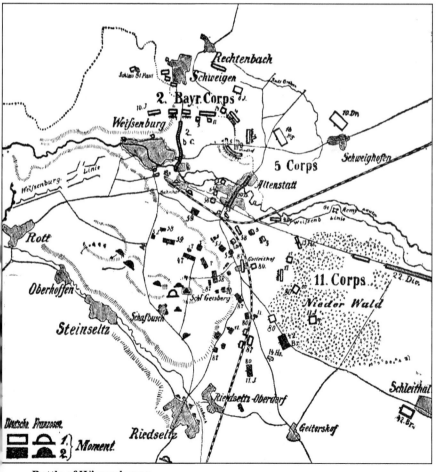

Battle of Wissembourg.

On the morning of Thursday 4 August, MacMahon's 2nd Division, some 8,600 men commanded by General Abel Douay, brother of General Félix Douay, was the first to make contact with leading elements of the Prussian Third Army, 130,000 men strong. During the night, while the rain was bucketing down, Douay's division had taken up positions on the heights west of Wissembourg, just a few hundred metres from the Franco-German border. Meanwhile, on the German side of the border, without being noticed by the French cavalry that had supposedly scouted the area, the German Third Army was massing; an unequal struggle was about to take place.

At about 8.00 am, during morning coffee, shells started raining down on Wissembourg and the surprised French troops; Prussian and Bavarian troops made for the city. The French, quickly manning the ramparts of the old and de-classified fortress town, started to put up a stiff fight, causing many casualties with their superior Chassepot rifles. It was also the first time the Germans had faced the power of the mitrailleuse, as volley after volley was fired into the dense masses of attacking Bavarians. After the war, a Bavarian officer wrote that '...few are wounded by the

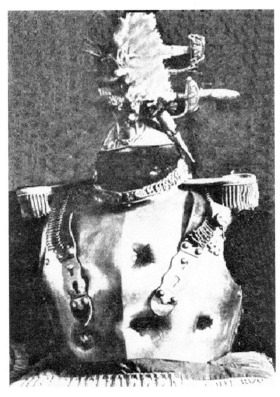

Body armour after receiving a volley of machine-gun fire.

mitrailleuse. If it hits you, you're dead.' The reason for this was that the gun did not traverse like the machine guns we know from World War One; the aim was fixed on a single goal. When you were hit, it could well be by twenty-five lead bullets thirteen millimeters in diameter (approx. 0.5 inches) simultaneously, almost like a shrapnel burst.

Although the French managed to inflict heavy casualties with their rapid-firing mitrailleuses, their defences began to crumble. At the end of the morning, while General Douay was inspecting the battlefield, he was blown from his horse by an exploding shell. He died instantly. Despite heavy resistance, around noon the French were forced to retreat in the direction of Spicheren in order to avoid the overwhelming advancing Germans and the threat of being surrounded. In spite of a heroic last stand at Château de Geisberg by a few hundred French regulars and Turcos (Turcos: a nickname given to colonial troops from Algeria who had fought outstandingly well alongside the Turks in the Crimean War), having run out of ammunition, they were forced to surrender at about 2.00 pm. It was rather disheartening for the French troops who had been defending the town so desperately that it was the inhabitants of Wissenbourg who surrendered to the enemy; they hoisted the white flag, opened the gates and lowered the drawbridge to let the Germans in. In this way they were hoping to prevent the destruction of their town. It left the French garrison of 300 soldiers no other choice but to surrender. Soon

The heroic last stand at Château Geisberg.

column after column of German troops poured into the burning town, looking for food, drink and loot.

After a very hot and sunny day, the weather changed for the worse. It was now pelting with rain which, and as a result of the thousands of feet tramping over the surface, very soon turned the roads, just very basic tracks that were hardly two metres wide, into quagmires. The planned German pursuit of MacMahon's 2nd Division literally became bogged down because of the awful weather.

When MacMahon finally heard about the disaster, he ordered the survivors to retreat to the Frœschwiller-Wœrth line, a natural wall of hills and easily defensible. From here he thought it would be easier to unite with the Army of the Rhine and Failly's V Corps. The weather had seriously hampered the French retreat, but at least it bought them some time as the Germans had stopped their pursuit altogether.

The German victory over the small French garrison at Wissembourg was the start of the invasion of France. This first major encounter resulted in the loss of 274 German dead and 1,886 wounded. The French lost 2,300 killed and wounded, nearly half of them prisoners.

Saturday 6 August, the Battle of Spicheren and Forbach.
Shocked by the German victory at Wissembourg, Napoleon, looking ill and in excruciating pain from his bladder stone, suddenly realized that the French army was much too large for one person to command and so he decided to divide it into two separate wings. This was a wise decision, but it came too late as the overall command structure of the army had already been thrown into complete disarray by Napoleon's previous decisions. He assigned the northern wing, which he now called the Army of the Rhine, in the Metz (Lorraine) area, to Marshal Bazaine. Their relationship had deteriorated over the previous days, because to Bazaine, the proud and professional soldier, the Emperor's decisions were puzzling to say the very least. In fact, most of the other generals thought Napoleon was a nuisance to have on the battlefield.

The south-eastern wing of Alsace would be Marshal MacMahon's responsibility, who immediately put his rank to use by ordering General Failly's V Corps to join him, hoping to stem the German invasion as soon as possible. Failly, however, was afraid this would weaken his defences on the southern end of France's border and decided to send just one division; this was to turn out to be a disastrous decision. Within French ranks the first protests had already sounded; long marches, the lack of sleep and food had already had taken their toll on morale.

The German First Army, under General von Steinmetz, advanced west from Saarbrücken and attacked Frossard's II Corps (the 2nd Division was now commanded by General Pellé) once again at Spicheren and Forbach. Frossard managed to repulse early German attacks, but the French came under increasing pressure on their flanks as more Germans arrived. While the French soldiers at Spicheren were desperately trying to stem the tide, Bazaine refused to send reinforcements. Frossard, greatly outnumbered and his men suffering greatly from the intense barrage that the German gunners were putting them under, was unsurprisingly forced to retreat. Finally, when the German Second Army, under Prince Friedrich Karl of Prussia, came to the aid of their compatriots they routed the French in a blazing attack. It is worth

General von Steinmetz, 1796-1877.

mentioning that the failure of the French commanders to support each other (Failly failed to support MacMahon at Wœrth in the south on the same day) was one of the main causes of the French losing the war. The Battle of Spicheren was the second French defeat.

The German victory compelled Frossard to withdraw in the direction of Metz, where he hoped to join up with Bazaine's Army. The Germans

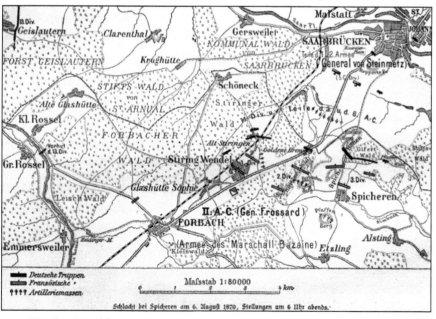

The Battles of Saarbrücken, Spicheren and Forbach.

lost 223 officers and 4,648 men, amongst the dead a general who, somewhat ironically, gloried in the name of von Francois.

Although ending in a German victory, Moltke could have destroyed II Corps if General Steinmetz had not operated on his own initiative. Steinmetz and his Army were to act as a reserve and were not supposed to attack. Impatient and hungry for the fight and the honour of the battlefield, he had sent in General Kameke to beat the Second Army to the punch, thus attacking too early and before the Second Army had arrived in full force. As a result of this impulsive act, seventy per cent of the French escaped being encircled and went on to live to fight

Prince Friedrich Karl of Prussia.

another day. Prince Friedrich Karl, the Army's commander, Moltke and the High Command were all flabbergasted by Steinmetz's impetuousity, which ruined their plans. Amazingly, despite his insubordination, Steinmetz kept his commission as commander of the First Army, mainly due to being a friend of the king's and his popularity among the troops.

Napoleon and Marshal Le Bœuf, who were supervising the army from their headquarters in Metz, ordered Frossard to withdraw closer to Metz, thus leaving a massive gap between Failly's V and MacMahon's I Corps, which had been engaged in heavy fighting with the German Third Army in Frœschwiller and Wœrth.

Marshal Le Bœuf, 1809-1888.

Saturday 6 August, the Battle of Frœschwiller-Wœrth.

On Friday 5 August, on General Frossard's advice, MacMahon's four infantry divisions of I Corps took up position on Frœschwiller Ridge. Here, some forty kilometres north of Strasbourg, he believed that he would be in a position to defend himself or to attack the German flank if they tried to pass him. All day troops had been arriving at Frœschwiller in the rain. When night fell, the hungry and rain soaked soldiers started to pillage the town.

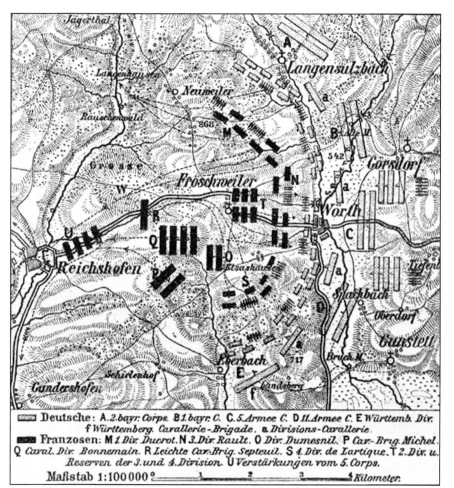

Deutsche: A.2.bayr. Corps. B.1.bayr. C. C.5.Armee C. D.11.Armee C. E.Württemb. Dir. f Württemberg. Cavallerie-Brigade. a Divisions-Cavallerie. Franzosen: M 1 Dir. Ducrot. N 3.Dir. Raoult. O Dir. Dumesnil. P Cav.-Brig. Michel. Q Caval.Dir. Bonnemain. R Leichte Cav.Brig. Septeuil. S 4.Dir. de Lortique. T 2.Dir. u. Reserven der 3.und 4.Division. U Verstärkungen vom 5.Corps.
Maßstab 1:100 000 ? 1 2 3 4 Kilometer.

The German and French positions at Frœschwiller-Wœrth.

McMahon did not expect there to be any fighting on Saturday so he allowed his troops, about 48,000 men, to have a rest as well as ordering that every man should be given double rations. However, the latest intelligence indicated that the Prussian Third Army, commanded by Crown Prince Friedrich, some 130,000 men, were massing on the German side of the border. Generals Ducrot and Raoult tried to convince MacMahon to withdraw to the Vosges passes, but he declined. Expecting Failly's V Corps to arrive at any moment, he decided to stand and fight, if battle would occur that day.

The Germans established themselves on the east bank of the River Sauer while the French Army, in much smaller numbers, took up position on the Frœschwiller Plateau between Langensoultzbach and Morsbronn-les-Bains. Crown Prince Friedrich thought that it would be too costly to take the French positions in a frontal assault and needed more time to assemble his troops and to prepare the attack by going round the flanks. The attack was originally planned for 7 August.

Neither side had intended to fight on the 6th, but skirmishes near the river at Wœrth provoked a major action. Frœschwiller was therefore an impromptu battle; more and more troops from both sides were thrown into the fray and were engaged in a violent battle all day long. At first the French, on the high ground, managed to hold the Germans back and severely punished any attempt to storm their positions. But when the Germans started massing their batteries along the hills east of the Sauer River they quickly established artillery dominance and the first cracks in the French defence became visible.

Despite strong resistance, the right wing of the French Army was overrun and at around 1.00 pm the Germans captured the village of Morsbronn. In an attempt to recapture Morsbronn, MacMahon made the mistake of launching the 9th Curassiers of General Michel's Cavalry Brigade over highly unfavourable terrain covered with hop plants and vines. The French crack cavalry unit was mown down by Prussian snipers and peppered by grapeshot. Struggling to descend the slopes and greatly hindered by tree trunks and the wooden poles that supported the hops, the cuirassiers who managed to enter Morsbronn were butchered in the streets by fire at close range; the few who survived the onslaught

Artist's impression of Morsbronn.

surrendered. Soon it became clear that the French had been forced to give up the plan of retaking the village altogether. One source reported that only twenty-two out of the 800 of Michel's men survived the charge. The Germans did not waste time; when they felt that the tide of the battle was turning in their favour, they quickly launched a counter-attack, quickly taking Elsasshausen and then threatening the road to Frœschwiller. In the meantime, a now very worried MacMahon, who was watching the battle from the top of a hill through his telescope, was counting on the arrival of Failly's V Corps. Several head-on counter-attacks were ordered; both sides suffered appalling losses. The French fought like lions but in the end they were outflanked and out-manoeuvred by the Germans.

At around 3.30 pm, a desperate MacMahon launched four elite regiments of General Bonnemain's heavy cavalry against the advancing Germans in order to provide cover for his retreating army; but once again the result was a disaster and it cost the French 500 men. The attack of the 1st Regiment of Algerian Tirailleurs (sharpshooters) nonetheless slowed the German advance with a daring assault in which they, briefly, managed to retake Elzasshausen; but they were forced to retreat by a hail of shells and in a short time they lost some 800 men. By 4.00 pm the French had been boxed in on three sides; it was only a matter of time before the Bavarians turned the left flank. The battle continued into the village of Frœschwiller, which suffered intense bombing and fell to the Germans at 5.00 pm.

The French Army retreated in disorder to Reichshoffen and Niederbronn, to the west. MacMahon and General Ducrot, their uniforms scarred with bullets, were amongst the last ones to leave the battlefield. Between Reichshoffen

General Bonnemain, 1814-1885.

and Niederbronn MacMahon finally met up with the division that Failly had sent to support him, but it was too little too late; the battle had already been lost. That night it dawned on MacMahon that not stopping the German invasion there and then might mean that the war was effectively lost. He was right.

As in previous battles, during the Battle of Frœschwiller-Wœrth the Germans succeeded in separating the northern and southern flanks of the French Army. Learning of this third German victory in a row, Napoleon and Le Bœuf were compelled to withdraw their troops to defend Metz and the surrounding area, a disastrous decision, as soon became evident.

At the conclusion of this first major battle, the French had suffered huge losses; there were 10,400 dead and wounded and 9,200 Frenchmen had been taken prisoner, including General Raoult. The Germans lost 10,500 dead, wounded and missing. For many of the wounded help came too late; the terrible wounds inflicted by the lead bullets caused many men to die from infection and loss of blood. Among amputees there was an almost 80 per cent mortality rate. Numerous mass graves and tombs were dug; the civilians of Wœrth and Frœschwiller were 'honoured' with the gruesome task of burying the dead. Without distinction, the French and German dead were thrown into the same pit; horses

General Raoult, 1810-1870.

were buried where they had died. The smell of the putrefying bodies that were lying exposed to the hot August sun was beyond description.

By now MacMahon's army was in full retreat; it was up to Marshall Bazaine to save not only the day but, unknown to him at the time, in fact the fate of France at Metz. Meanwhile, the Germans were taking possession of Alsace, ransacking every poor French village on their way westwards. The Germans thought that MacMahon's beaten army would join up with Bazaine in the Metz area, but in fact MacMahon had been ordered to retreat to Châlons Camp in order to regroup and to cover Paris. As MacMahon's troops scattered in all directions and tried to escape by all means to Châlons, the Germans lost them in the chase.

On 9 August the demoralized French troops learnt that theirs had not been the only defeat on the 6th; the defeat of General Frossard's troops at Spicheren and Forbach came as a devastating blow. The German First and Second Armies were now concentrating their energy on Bazaine's Army in Metz, while the bulk of the Third Army was on its way to Châlons to catch up with MacMahon. Part of the Third Army moved south, to Strasbourg.

Paris and politics.

Meanwhile things were deteriorating around Metz. With MacMahon's army effectively cut off from the Army of the Rhine and fleeing to Châlons, the situation was far from rosy. When news of these setbacks arrived in Paris, the Empire was shaken to its foundations; Ollivier declared Paris to be in a state of siege and ordered all men under thirty to report for military service. Angry mobs were barely kept in control by the troops. Public opinion in France had turned against the government and on the evening of 9 August the Ollivier administration was forced to step down in favour of a new one that it was hoped could lead France through the crisis. General Cousin de Monteauban, better known as Palikao, the former Minister of War, became France's new Prime Minister.

On the same day, Napoleon was forced by the new French Government to give up the command of the army; Bazaine replaced him at the helm. On 11 August, a reluctant Napoleon was ordered to sack his chief of staff, Marchal Le Bœuf; it was hoped that by replacing the top command the French would regain the initiative. Two days later Napoleon left the fortress of Metz but remained in the area.

In the meantime, the Germans surge continued into France at considerable speed; by the time that Bazaine issued his first orders, the Second Army was bypassing Metz in the south and were in the process of wheeling north again, while Steinmetz's First Army was approaching the city head on. Two mighty pincers were threatening to encircle Metz while the French were quarrelling in Paris.

Marshal Bazaine wasted a full week by allowing his army to stay in Metz; only on 14 August, eight days after the Battle of Spicheren/Forbach, did he order some troops out of Metz to take up defensive positions in the hills above St. Privat, Amanvillers and Gravelotte, north west of Metz, in order to cover the retreat, via Verdun, to Châlons. Other troops were still positioned to the east of the city, in the area between Mey and Borny; there were simply too many French soldiers in the area and it took two days to march them through Metz.

Sunday 14 August: The Battle of Borny.
This battle was, like Frœschwiller, not a battle that had been planned by Bazaine or Steinmetz but was once more a consequence of aggressive subordinates taking the initiative. In the late afternoon, as Bazaine's troops were taking up positions on the right bank of the River Moselle, General Goltz of Steinmetz's VII Corps started the attack from the woods of Borny. The French and German troops smashed into each other and the fighting continued well into the evening. However, it was a half-hearted battle; due to lack of decisive leadership the fighting petered out. In spite of this, casualties on both sides were very heavy: 3,409 French and 4,906 Germans. Both sides claimed victory. To the Germans, this battle confirmed that the bulk of Bazaine's army was still in Metz; it also slowed down the possible retreat to Verdun/Châlons. Moltke quickly

The battles around Metz are marked A, B and C.

ordered the Second Army to speed up the encirclement of Metz; this was his chance to deal with the French Army of the Rhine once and for all.

Tuesday 16 August: The Battle of Mars-la-Tour
On Tuesday 16 August, Napoleon, sick, tired and looking very unhealthy, left for Gravelotte, where he stayed at the local inn. During his last

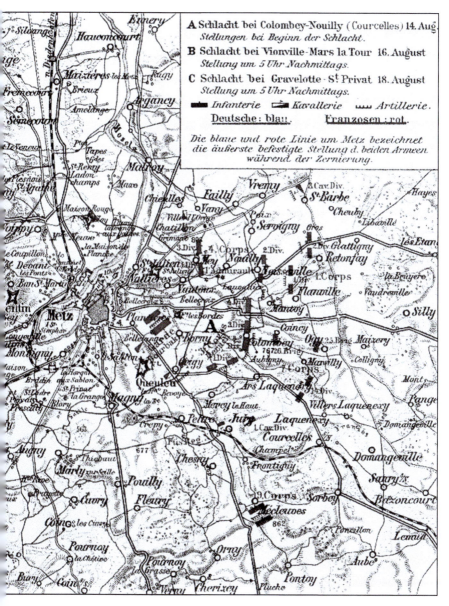

meeting with Bazaine, he urged him to retreat via the Verdun Road so as to join up with MacMahon in Châlons; he thought this would be the perfect place from which to execute a fighting retreat to Paris.

While the columns of Bazaine's army were leaving Metz at a snail's pace, a German cavalry patrol, led by Captain Oskar von Blumenthal, came across them. Believing that it was the rearguard (in fact it was the advance guard) of the retreating Army of the Rhine, Friedrich Karl sent a group of 30,000 men of the advanced III Corps of the Second Army, under General Constantin von Alvensleben, with orders to cut them off. At around 10.00 am, they located the French Army near Vionville, east of Mars-la-Tour. Little did they know that they were facing 130,000 French soldiers and that they were outnumbered more than four to one. The Germans launched an attack on the French advance guard. Chaotic fighting broke out all along the line, both sides inflicting a large number of casualties on each another.

The move that resolved the situation was a daring German cavalry charge, commanded by Major General von Bredow, arguably, the last successful great cavalry charge of European warfare. General von Alvensleben, harassed by French artillery each time he redeployed his forces following a French attack, with his infantry reserves exhausted and fearing that his shaky left flank was about to be charged by

Major General von Bredow, 1814-1890.

French cavalry, sent a message to the commander of the nearby 12th Cavalry Brigade, von Bredow, demanding that he silence the French artillery and forestall an enemy cavalry charge with one of his own.

Realising that 'it will cost what it will', von Bredow took his time in organizing his men which comprised the 7th Cavalry, 19th Dragoons, 16th Uhlans and the 12th Cavalry Brigade (von Bredow). In what would become known in history as 'von Bredow's Death Ride', the cavalrymen rode out from the Prussian lines at 2.00 pm, von Bredow using the terrain and gun smoke to keep their movements hidden from French observers until the very last moment. Bursting into view some 1,000 metres from the French lines, the Prussian cavalry charged into and broke through

General von Alvensleben, 1809-1892.

the French artillery lines, causing widespread panic and scattering Canrobert's gunners and soldiers in all directions. Two brigades of French cavalry attempted to counter-charge into Von Bredow's flank and rear, but, very conveniently for the Germans, this attempt was disrupted by Canrobert's panic-stricken infantry, who were shooting willy-nilly and just gunned down any cavalryman they could see without making any distinction between the two sides.

Having silenced the French artillery, neutralized the French cavalry and panicked the French infantry, von Bredow's own brigade managed to extricate itself and withdrew to their own lines. Of the 800 horsemen who had started out, however, only 420 returned.

Incredibly, and despite being massively outnumbered, the 30,000 Germans kept the French busy for the whole day and ultimately ended in the rout of the entire Army of the Rhine and the capture of Vionville. Once again, German bravado and confidence prevailed over Bazaine's indecision. Any attempt to escape to the west was blocked for the moment, but the encirclement of the French was not yet complete; there was still a chance of an escape between Gravelotte and St. Privat. However, the French had to move quickly if they wanted to take the opportunity. During the battle of Mars-la-Tour, each side suffered an estimated 16,000 casualties.

Thursday 18 August: The Battles of Gravelotte and St. Privat.

On Wednesday 17 August, Bazaine withdrew his army to a line of hills running north-south, between the walled village of St. Privat and Gravelotte, a few miles to the north west of Metz. The French were now facing west, towards their intended line of retreat, i.e. Verdun. Early on the morning of 18 August, the Germans were unaware that the French lay on their right flank as they deployed parallel to the road from Mars-la-Tour to Metz, facing north. When the French positions were discovered, several German units turned 90° to the east to face the French lines. Moltke was forced to send his troops directly against the well-positioned French and only the indecisiveness of Bazaine permitted Moltke to turn what initially seemed likely to end, at best, as a draw into a victory.

The northern sector of the French line, around St. Privat, did not budge and the riflemen wrought havoc on the German frontal attacks. However, at nightfall the French were ordered to retire to Metz. The southern sector of the French line, situated behind a deep ravine and prepared trenches, had pulverized the German assaults directed against it. Moltke was therefore totally flabbergasted when, instead of counter-attacking in order to re-open the road to Verdun, Bazaine used the night to pull back to Metz.

Once more, the number of casualties had been appalling; the German lost more than 20,000 men at Gravelotte, French casualties amounted to 13,000.

During the battles fought on 14, 16 and 18 August, the French losses were 2,719 dead, 17,667 wounded and 9,258 missing or captured: a total of 29,644 men. The Germans losses were even worse: 10,848 dead,

French curassiers, heavily armed cavalry equipped with body armour.

28,440 wounded and 1,630 missing or captured, a total of 40,918 casualties. This shocking number of casualties (a combined total of 70,562) was the result of mechanized warfare. Machine guns and rapid firing breech-loading cannon made it possible to kill and maim on an unprecedented scale, something that became commonplace during the First World War. (On 1 July 1916, for example, the opening day of the infamous Battle of the Somme, the British forces suffered an estimated 57,470 casualties, including 19,240 fatalities.)

19 August-27 October: the Siege of Metz.
Although the German losses in manpower were considerably larger than the French, (who claimed victory at St. Privat on the basis of counting the number of casualties), they had accomplished their purpose of encircling Bazaine's Army of the Rhine and were the tactical victors of the battle. Moltke only used a small part of his forces (Second Army, commanded by Friedrich Karl of Prussia) to confine Bazaine's troops, a staggering 180,000 men, in Metz. He was able to order the remainder to advance north along the right bank of the River Meuse, where they eventually participated in the attack on MacMahon's Army of Châlons at Sedan.

During the first days of the Siege of Metz, the Germans launched several attacks in order to try to get a foothold in the city, but to no avail; murderous Chassepot and cannon fire forced them to retreat time and again. An anonymous English officer and eyewitness of the siege wrote that Metz was:

'Surrounded on all sides but the north by a vast, perfectly flat and almost open plain; an enemy advancing to assault would, for some miles, be exposed to a murderous fire from the guns of the fortress, with scarcely a chance of replying with any effect: the few who survived the ordeal would, on arriving at the foot of the walls, be delayed by obstacles under such fire of Chassepots that none could remain alive. The northern ridge, it is true, commands the town but it is so strongly fortified and held by the French [not surprising; never was the garrison as large as during the siege] that there is, we suspect, little opening for success in that quarter. If, on the other hand, the Prussians were to besiege the place in form, they might ultimately effect its capture but the loss of men they would be liable to in establishing their batteries and pushing forward their advances would probably exceed that of a hard-fought battle.

The Prussians themselves are the first to recognise the facts. But why, they say, should we expose ourselves to the risk of heavy losses and failure, when, by watching the fortress with the large army we have now available and patiently starving it out, we can attain the same object almost without losing a hundred men.'

At the end of August, Bazaine undertook two half-hearted attempts to break the siege in order to team up with MacMahon; first at Noisseville and again at Bellevue; but he was repulsed each time. When the news reached Metz of the defeat of Napoleon and MacMahon at Sedan, morale plummeted; all hope was lost now and the fall of the Empire was just a matter of time.

During the siege of Metz there was a growing feeling of bitter hatred towards the German army due to the mounting number of French casualties caused by hunger.

'Look, there is their [French] picket sheltered to the rear of it [a French earthwork]. Do you see the different sets of sentries dodging each other? And sure enough, after carefully examining the ground, we discovered in the straggling copses below, connected together by hedgerows, both French and Prussian

Part of the defences at Metz after Bazaine's surrender.

vedettes and sentinels skirting the fences, turning sharp round the corners and endeavouring to kill one another. This kind of murderous work was continually going on, our informant assured us, and the aggregate number of lives thus uselessly lost was considerable. Indeed, nations seem of late years to have retrograded to a marked extent in the amenities and chivalrous courtesies of warfare.'

Adding to the terrible conditions inside the fortress walls of Metz, the city's hospitals and barracks, which had been hastily adapted to their new function, held no less than 15,000 sick and wounded; food and water were rationed to a point that there was hardly enough to survive, but just sufficient to prevent people from dying. First, the horses were eaten and not much later neither a cat nor a dog was to be found in the city. As a last resort in the search for protein, people started to eat rats, which heavily effected morale. In short, the German siege started to bear fruit. At the end of October the population of Metz and the soldiers wanted Bazaine and the Metz War Council to open negotiations secretly with the enemy. This eventually led to the capitulation of the city, officially signed at the Château de Frescaty, and which came into effect at 4.00 pm on 27 October 1870. The Prussians offered the honours of war to the defeated French Army but, contrary to usual practice, Bazaine refused the honour.

Bazaine and his army marched off into captivity; the Second Army was now free to besiege Paris. For Bazaine, personally, things got even worse; the leaders of the new Republic labelled Bazaine a traitor and sentenced him to death. It was felt that his surrender and the freeing up of enemy troops prevented a (very imaginative!) victory against the Prussians in the Loire. However, the sentence was commuted and he died in poverty in exile in Spain, fighting to his death to restore his good name, which to the present day is held in high regard by the Foreign Legion. On 29 October, after the evacuation of the Army of the Rhine and the sick and wounded, General von Kammern triumphantly entered Metz.

According to Moltke's autobiography, published in 1892 (*Zur Lebensgeschichte des General-Feldmarschalls Grafen Helmuth von Moltke*), the French lost 167,000 enlisted men and 6,000 officers, as well as 20,000 sick after the surrender of Metz. Material losses amounted to 622 field guns, seventy-two mitrailleuses and 260,000 rifles. The Germans lost an estimated 5,500 men and 240 officers killed and wounded during the siege.

The events in and around Metz in August 1870 will be described in more detail in a future book in the Battleground Europe Series.

A Prussian artillery unit at Metz.

CHAPTER 3

The Army of Châlons,
17-28 August

The retreat from Frœschwiller to Châlons Camp.
On Thursday 4 August, at the border garrison town of Wissembourg, the German Third Army, led by Crown Prince Friedrich Wilhelm of Prussia, defeated the forward division of MacMahon's army, commanded by General Abel Douay, who was killed during the fighting. Two days later, on Saturday 6 August, at the Battle of Frœschwiller, named after the town around which the battle was fought, the French again suffered the ignominy of defeat.

Marshal MacMahon had waited in vain for reinforcements from General Failly's V Corps during the fighting at Frœschwiller. He had started out with 48,000 men but by the end of the day that number had been whittled down to 27,000. The numerically superior Prussian Third Army, 80,000 strong, lost around 10,000 men.

General Abel Douay, 1809-1870.

When the news of the reverse at Frœschwiller reached Paris, angry mobs went out into the streets; revolution was once more in the air. Officially, Empress Eugénie's message to the public was that MacMahon's army had merely retreated to a second line and that everything would be all right in the end. Little did she know that within four weeks the republican revolution would triumph and that the Bonapartes would be exiled from France. As a result of the French defeat, MacMahon ordered the tattered remains of his army to retreat to Châlons with orders to reorganize and replenish at the army base at Châlons Camp near Châlons-sur-Marne, capital of the Champagne-Ardennes region. From here,

General de Failly, 1810-1892.

Looting Prussians in Alsace.

MacMahon was ordered to defend Paris as the southern route to the French capital was now wide open.

In the meantime, the Germans could not quite believe what had happened; they had expected the remains of MacMahon's army to retreat to the north in order to join up with the northern branch of the Army of the Rhine in the area around the City of Metz and to launch a counter attack. Instead, MacMahon and his army had deserted the province of Alsace altogether. While MacMahon and his beaten army retreated in disarray further west into French territory, the Prussian Third Army, now that they had free rein in Alsace, captured town after town, pillaging and looting the area. They generally adopted a policy of anything that was not nailed down was taken and what could not be taken was set on fire; as usual, women, children and old people suffered the most. The Germans were hoping to force the fleeing French army to surrender but the problem was that the remnants of the French army had scattered in all directions. Fortunately for the French, the Germans had soon lost track of the main force. Contradictory orders, poor command systems, lack of food and other badly needed supplies hampered any prospect of a smooth and orderly withdrawal of the French army. Many of the wounded fortunate enough to evade capture by the Germans died under appalling conditions in improvised hospitals. Exhausted doctors operated without anaesthetics or used spirits for that purpose, when available. A simple flesh wound could be fatal without treatment and as a consequence many soldiers died of blood poisoning. The indecision of the French High Command communicated itself to the troops, who could not understand why they were marching away from the frontier and the enemy. Marches were badly organized, with men having to stand in ranks for hours on end while waiting their turn to join a column. Many soldiers had lost or discarded all their equipment in the aftermath of battle. Tormented by hunger, soldiers increasingly resorted to begging and looting. Finally, two weeks later and after endless delays I and V Corps arrived at Châlons Camp.

On Saturday 6 August, General Félix Douay, commander of VII Corps, received the devastating news of the disaster at Frœschwiller and the death of his brother, General Abel Douay. Although VII Corps was not under direct threat from the Germans, this news caused morale to dwindle immediately; chaos reigned among the ranks and again many soldiers discarded their equipment, rifles and ammunition. As the most southern section of MacMahon's Army, they protected the fortified cities of Mulhouse and Belfort. With the risk of being cut from MacMahon's main force and without any protection on their flanks, it was decided that this army was also to retreat to the Châlons/Reims area. In the south, the fortress town of Belfort was garrisoned and the rest of the VII Corps was marched off to different railheads and transported to the rear.

General Félix Douay, 1816-1879.

On Tuesday 16 August the official order came that they were to join the remnants of I and V Corps at Châlons Camp. Finally, on Saturday 20 August, most of the troops were entrained and headed west.

As if the collapse of MacMahon's Army was not bad enough for the French, on 20 August it became known that two days earlier Marshal Bazaine's Army of the Rhine had lost the strategic Battle of St. Privat. Bazaine and his 180,000 soldiers, plus equipment, had retreated to the fortress town of Metz where they quickly became besieged by 300,000 Prussian troops. Consequently, the Army of the Rhine was renamed the Army of Metz by the French High Command. Before Bazaine's retreat to Metz and MacMahon's retreat to the west, the German High Command had feared that the two French armies would unite, thus forcing the Prussians to a standstill. Although Moltke would have preferred to encircle the whole French Army at Metz, he quickly adapted to the new

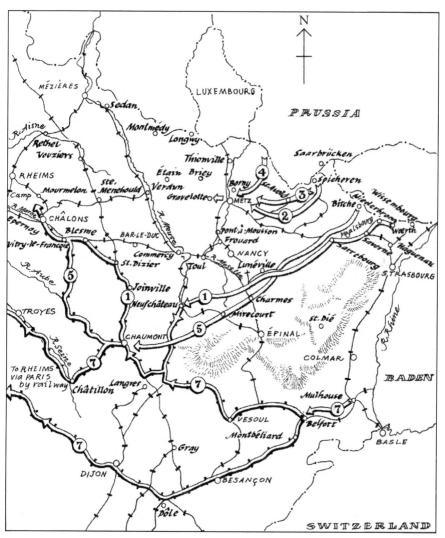

The French retreat. (John and Matthew Cook)

situation: he could besiege Bazaine's army in Metz with only a fraction of the troops he had at his disposal. The remainder of Crown Prince Friedrich Wilhelm's Third Army was completely free to manoeuvre and could, without the risk of Bazaine attacking the Prussians from the rear, either seek confrontation with MacMahon's Army in the open field in Châlons-sur-Marne or before Paris. The French invasion of Germany that had started on Tuesday 2 August had completely backfired; barely three weeks later the French High Command had to come up with a plan to save France.

Marshal MacMahon

Marshal Marie Esme Patrice Maurice, Count de MacMahon, Duke of Magenta, the son of Maurice François MacMahon and his wife, Pelagie Riquet de Caraman, was born on 13 July 1808, in the Château de Sully, in southern Burgundy (not to be confused with the Château de Sully, about fifty miles south of Paris). Maurice François and Pelagie had a very large family, seventeen children; Patrice was the sixteenth. As the name suggests, MacMahon was of Irish descent. His grandfather, Jean-Baptiste de MacMahon, was created Marquis de MacMahon and Marquis d'Equilly by King Louis XV in 1750. Château de Sully remains in the possession of the MacMahon family.

Marshal MacMahon, 1808-1893.

At the end of the seventeenth century the MacMahons were supporters of James II, King of England and Ireland (James VII of Scotland), the last Catholic monarch of Great Britain, who was deposed in 1688 by the Protestant William of Orange in the Glorious Revolution; William was married to Mary, James' eldest daughter. The ensuing struggle between James and William, the Williamite-Jacobite War in Ireland (1689-1691) was the one serious attempt James made to win back his crown. The Treaty of Limerick, signed on 3 October 1691, brought the war to an end. The Jacobites (Catholics) believed that they had negotiated a treaty that guaranteed the rights of their people; in theory, the Jacobite Irish were to recover their property but the English failed to honour the terms of the treaty. Instead, they introduced the Penal Laws, stripping Irish Catholics of their land, their right to education and their right to vote. Catholics were also barred from the legal profession and from becoming Members of Parliament; the Penal Laws even went so far as to prohibit Catholics from owning a horse worth over £5.

'The Flight of the Wild Geese', the emigration of the defeated soldiers of the Jacobite army to Europe, began in the last decade of the seventeenth century and continued on into the eighteenth. In 1749, members of the MacMahon family of Dooradoyle, Limerick, moved to France.

After a carefree childhood, Patrice MacMahon was educated at the Lycée Louis-le-Grand. At the end of two years of specialized training at St-Cyr Military Academy in Paris, he graduated in 1827. The Academy, founded by Napoleon in 1802, was the most important and

The prestigious Special Military School of St. Cyr.

prestigious officers' school in the country. St-Cyr Academy was an educational institution for the nobility and rich upper classes; its graduates were trained to a high and professional level and formed the backbone of the French officer corps. After his graduation MacMahon was commissioned as a second lieutenant in the 4th Hussars but was sent to Algeria as a junior officer with the 20th Infantry Regiment.

MacMahon served as aide-de-camp to General Achard and consequently participated in the occupation of Algiers in 1830. From 1834-1854 he was posted almost permanently in Algeria; in 1837 he was wounded during an assault on the city of Constantine. In December 1841 he was placed in command of a battalion of light infantry. Two years later, he was designated commander of the 2nd Foreign Regiment of the Foreign Legion. By 1848 MacMahon was brigadier general and in 1852 was promoted to divisional general.

In March 1854, MacMahon was sent to the Crimea. Here, the French fought alongside the Sardinians and the British and Ottoman Empires against the Russians in a war that started in the autumn of 1853 and continued to February 1856 Although it ended in an Allied victory, it had cost France dearly, with the loss of some 100,000 men, dead and wounded, two thirds of whom died of disease, mainly cholera.

By the time the war ended in February 1856, MacMahon's star had risen rapidly and he was offered a position at senior level in the French army. However, he declined, preferring to return to Algeria instead.

However, he served as a Senator of the Second Empire from 1856 until 1870, when it collapsed following the defeat at Sedan

After participating in several successful military incidents during the Second Italian War of Independence, as commander of the Second Corps MacMahon led the French to victory at Magenta on 4 June, 1859; he received a battlefield promotion to the rank of Marshal of France. From 1864 until the outbreak of hostilities between France and Prussia and her German allies, MacMahon occupied the post of Governor-General of the French colony of Algeria. Napoleon III bestowed on him the title Duke of Magenta in 1860; in 1864 the title was confirmed as hereditary.

During the Franco-Prussian War MacMahon seemed to have lost his touch; his indecision first lost France the province of Alsace; a few weeks later, he and his Army were encircled by the German Army at Sedan. MacMahon was wounded in fighting in the hamlet of La Moncelle as the French attempted to fight their way out of the town.

After Sedan, MacMahon led the Army that defeated the Paris Commune in 1871, see chapter 7. In May 1873 he succeeded Adolphe Thiers when he was elected second President of the French Third Republic (1875-1879). After many disputes with the Republicans, MacMahon resigned and retired to private life. On 17 October 1893, the eighty-five year old Marshal of France died at Château de la Fôret in the valley of the Loire. The château, which passed to MacMahon on his marriage in 1842, remains in the possession of the MacMahon family. He was buried with full state honours in the crypt of Les Invalides, Paris.

Château de la Fôret, MacMahon's home on the Loire, where he died in 1893.

The creation of the Garde Mobile.

Although there was conscription into the army, it was not, in reality, universal; the sons of the middle and upper classes had the financial wherewithal to be able to avoid conscription by purchasing exemptions in a system known as *replacement*. As Minister of War, Marshal Adolphe Niel (1802-1869), was in charge of reforming the French army. In December 1866, Napoleon announced the creation of the *Garde Mobile*. It was intended to bolster the professional army in time of need; in theory, the Garde Mobile could comprise 600,000 men. Niel, the thinker behind the Garde Mobile, who wished to conscript all those

General Adolphe Niel, 1802-1869.

who were avoiding official military service, came up with the plan of a people's army that would have fifteen days annually to train. To encourage the 'conscripts' and to reduce costs, none of these training days would go on all day so that the men could return home to sleep in their own bed! Needless to say, the quality of these amateur soldiers was questionable at the very least.

The French generals and the *Corps Législatif*, the lower, elected part of the French legislature, which enacted or rejected proposed legislation, were not happy with Napoleon's plan of an untrained armed mob which would be responsible for the protection of France's fortress cities; many members preferred to enlarge and rely on an all-professional army. Therefore, it comes as no great surprise that only the minimum amount of the army budget was spent on equipment and training. As a result, the Garde Mobile was neither respected by nor popular amongst the people and quickly lost any authority it may ever have had.

In spite of all this, most of the important cities created a Garde Mobile that was commanded by local influential people. This created problems of its own, as for example a successful entrepreneur does not necessarily make a good officer of whatever rank. Another problem was that the Garde Mobile was hardly mobile; most of the time they were only permitted to operate in their own little sector within the safety of the walls of fortified cities.

When the Franco-Prussian War broke out, thousands of men who were called up to serve in the Garde Mobile were kitted out with second-rate equipment. Many of the men were unfamiliar with the new French Chassepot rifle, if issued a rifle at all. The 'People's Army' also lacked cohesion, training and respect for their superiors. According to the French historian, Léonce Rousset, when push came to shove, theoretically, around 80,000 men of the Garde Mobile and 330,000 other reservists were available to defend Paris. In reality, the Paris garrison came to just 150,000 men.

The French plan.

While the chaotic retreat of I and V Corps was taking place, the French Government decided that Napoleon III and his son, the Prince Imperial, who had left Bazaine's army before the encirclement of Metz, should return to Paris. This caused a sigh of relief amongst the French Army commanders in the field as Napoleon had mainly frustrated operations with his decisions or rather his indecisiveness. MacMahon and his troops were ordered to assist General Trochu, commander of all troops in Paris, with the defence of the capital. However, Empress Regent Eugénie, who feared for the dynasty, was deeply opposed to the plan. On the morning of Friday 19 August, after hearing of the disastrous news of the encirclement of Bazaine's army in Metz, the Empress, with the support of her ministers, decided that MacMahon should go to Bazaine's rescue in Metz.

The Prince Imperial, 1856-1879.

However, the Empress' main problem was that after the French newspapers had reported the French losses, the Siege of Metz and the withdrawal of MacMahon's army, republicans, revolutionaries and other opponents of the Empire became very active. Aware of the explosive political situation, the Empress considered the return of the Emperor to Paris undesirable, as this could be interpreted by the people that France had lost the war. Instead, she decided that for public opinion's sake a Napoleon Bonaparte belonged at the head of his troops to set the example, even if that meant certain death.

To bolster MacMahon's depleted army in Châlons, a new corps was created in Paris under the command of former Minister of War General Jules Trochu (1815-1896). On Monday 15 August the newly formed XII Corps and members of the Paris Garde Mobile departed for Châlons Camp. The next day, General Trochu met Napoleon, Prince Jerome, the Emperor's cousin, and Marshal MacMahon at the train station in Mourmelon. Here, it was decided that Trochu would be relieved as commander of XII Corps, and was to be tasked with the organization of the defence of the capital. Trochu went back to Paris and took most of the poorly armed and ill-disciplined Paris Garde Mobile with him. MacMahon was made First Commander of the troops at Châlons Camp

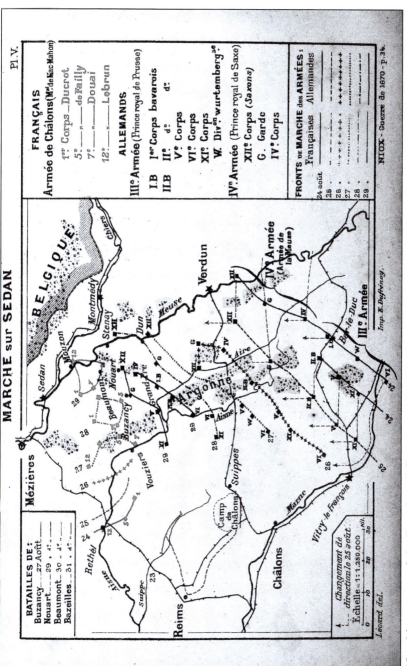

Marching routes of the French and German armies. The French were supposed to march to Montmédy. Cut off by the Germans time and again, they ended entrapped in Sedan.

but, strangely, remained under the command of Marshal Bazaine, who had virtually no contact with the outside world and by now had totally lost his grip on reality. The command of XII Corps was given to General Lebrun, who had accompanied the Emperor when he left Metz.

On Saturday 20 August, as soon as MacMahon's weary troops had received new equipment at Châlons Camp, they were on the move again; preparations were made for departure on the next day. To add to his misery, MacMahon had just learned that the spearhead of the German cavalry was only forty-five kilometres away from Châlons Camp. The 120,000 strong Army of Châlons (I and V Corps, reinforced by the fresh XII Corps) was to march off in the direction of Reims; it was considered easier to defend than Châlons Camp and was closer to Paris. From the Reims area MacMahon's army could either protect Paris or march in the direction of Verdun-Metz if necessary.

The columns of the Army of Châlons started the forty kilometres long march towards Reims on Sunday 21 August. The march was a disaster, mainly due to the endless traffic jams, the scorching heat of the August sun and the broken-down supply system, which combined to make the men even more exhausted and demoralized.

Meanwhile the Germans had not been wasting time. After Bazaine's Army of the Rhine had been surrounded at Metz, Prince Friedrich Karl's First Army were ordered to dig trenches and establish roadblocks; with every day that passed their defences grew stronger, thus making it more and more difficult for the French to break out. The Germans had also created a new army, the Fourth Army, under the command of Crown Prince Albert of Saxony; it became known as the Army of the Meuse. Together with Crown Prince Friedrich Wilhelm of Prussia's Third Army, they were to pursue the French and if possible strike the killer blow at Châlons in

Prince Albert of Saxony, 1828-1902.

order to defeat the tired and outnumbered French army and then continue on to Paris. On 21 August, the German Second, Fourth and Third Armies, about 250,000 men, moved westwards towards Verdun, St. Mihiel and Commercy. The Germans were well-informed as to the whereabouts of the French Army; incredibly, all they had to do was to read the lengthy reports about troop movements in the French newspapers.

The revised French plan.
No news had been received since the early morning of 19 August; on

Monday 22 August this lack of information made MacMahon decide to pull back from Paris. However, at 11.30 am he finally received a long-awaited message from Bazaine which had been smuggled out of Metz. It read: 'I am still counting on a breakthrough and plan to move north to Montmédy, eventually to reach Châlons. We are starting preparations.' MacMahon immediately changed his plans in order to go to Bazaine's aid and wrote back to him: *Received your message of 19 August. Am at Reims. Will march to Montmédy. In about two days I will have crossed the River Aisne.*

On that same day, at 4.00 pm, Napoleon III sent a telegram to General Palikao (1796-1878), the French Minister of War, to inform him of the situation. By now he was aware of the fact that the Germans were using French newspapers as a primary source of information. In order to divert German attention away from Châlons the Emperor ordered newspapers to publish the fake news that 150,000 men had broken through from Metz to St. Dizier.

The revised plan was to march the Army of Châlons north-north-east from Reims to Suippes, Vouziers and Buzancy in order to cross the River Meuse at Stenay and continue in the direction of the fortress city of Montmédy. Going at an average speed of twenty kilometres a day, theoretically, the River Meuse could be reached in five days. The plan was, in summary:

Napoleon III and the Prince Imperial surrounded by officers in Camp de Châlons, 1870.

51

Prussian troops marching towards Châlons.

1. Marshal Bazaine breaks through the encirclement of Metz and marches north to the city of Montmédy (180,000 men).
2. Marshal MacMahon immediately sets off to Montmédy to help Bazaine's army (120,000 men).
3. French reservists and the Garde Mobile under General Trochu protect Paris (theoretically over 400,000 men).

On the afternoon of Tuesday 23 August, MacMahon's Army of Châlons finally moved off and marched to Suippes, a distance of barely ten kilometres. The army moved at a snail's pace, while the Germans covered a minimum of twenty kilometres a day. After the last columns had left Châlons Camp, the remaining supplies were hastily set on fire to keep them out of German hands as the German V, VI and XI Corps were now less than thirty-five kilometres away. In spite of this, when the Germans arrived the next day they found many of the army supplies undamaged; by the next day, the French, who supposedly had rations for four days, were already running short of everything. It was another glaring example of extremely poor organization.

On Thursday 25 and Friday 26 August the French marched in the direction of Vouziers and Attingy, but by then they had realized that the German Third and Fourth Armies had abandoned their march to the west and were wheeling north in an attempt to intercept the Army of Châlons north of the Argonne to deny them access to the river crossings along the River Meuse. The Germans figured that the risk of a French attack on the German right flank or an attack from the rear was too great to ignore. Now the Germans marched north on both sides of the Argonne Forest and on both sides of the Meuse. If MacMahon did develop a plan his army would be crushed between two German armies.

When several German cavalry units were spotted, the French started to realize that the Germans were closing in on them from both sides of the Argonne. MacMahon and Napoleon III decided to split their army; VII and V Corps were to continue to Stenay to the east, while XII and I Corps and the Emperor were to try to cross the Meuse to the north, between Mouzon and Sedan.

At about the same time the situation in Metz started to deteriorate. According to an unknown German eyewitness account, a French spy who had escaped the encirclement of Metz was caught with Bazaine's plans.

'On 25 August, around midnight, General von Steinmetz [1796-1877] received a message that the next morning a secret messenger from Metz would be leaving for Paris with letters from Marshal Bazaine. The spy would be dressed as a Franciscan monk [sic – friar] and identifiable by a badge of the Geneva Convention (i.e., a red cross); by helping the wounded that lay around the besieged city, he hoped to use this to slip away undetected. So, von Steinmetz issued an accurate description of the impostor monk to Captain Poisl of the 13th Cavalry Regiment and to the guards who were promptly ordered to patrol the area.

Early in the morning four soldiers from Captain Poisl's regiment noticed a Franciscan Brother who was going in and out of the houses that had been commandeered as hospitals to take care of the wounded. He was taken into custody and brought before Captain Poisl who offered him a glass of wine. The 'monk' [sic – he was acting the part of a friar] started complaining about how he had been rudely interrupted while carrying out his devout work, whereupon Captain Poisl calmly told him a story about a monk accused of spying who had been hung just a few days earlier. Our 'monk' started to sweat, wished him a good day and told the captain that it was time to go, that duty called! Coolly, the captain answered that he first had to produce the letters otherwise he would kill him on the spot. Silently, and with shaking hands, he removed the double soles of his sandals and carefully withdrew the letters from their hiding place. The spy was removed to Spandau, Berlin.'

The three letters that the fake Franciscan monk had been carrying, fully informed the German High Command as to the situation in Metz and, more importantly, gave information about the direction MacMahon was going to take to come to Bazaine's aid. Of course, the high command did not hesitate in taking countermeasures.'

In the meantime, Bazaine himself did not do anything to break out of the Prussian siege of Metz. On the contrary; his generals advised him to remain inside the protection of the fort, arguing that there was barely enough ammunition for a break out and that morale was dwindling. The military authorities believed that the army should preserve themselves as a standing army to influence armistice negotiations, as the ill-informed generals expected Paris to be taken by the Germans any day. This defeatist attitude spread like wildfire amongst the upper commanders and the lower ranks and, apart from one half-hearted attempt to break through the German blockade on 31 August, it resulted in total lethargy in the garrison. Bazaine's surprising inactivity was a great gift to Moltke, who now had time to strengthen his position around Metz and to intensify the hunt for MacMahon.

Friday 26 August 1870: First blood of the Garde Mobile.

German reporter, Felix Dahn, recorded:

'Marching through the pretty Champagne region. After torrential rain the sun came out again from behind the clouds while we were marching from village to village. When finally the order to stop was given and we, with happy hearts, were making ourselves ready for the night, a messenger arrived. Shortly after, the officers sent out guards to act as lookouts on all access roads to the camp. We were all wondering why; for all we knew the enemy was still miles away at Châlons.

Later, we learnt that the day before and only a few kilometres from this place a Prussian vanguard had been involved in heavy fighting with an armed mob of around 800 civilians; thirty-three were killed and one hundred or so seriously wounded. I decided to take a look. After a while, I came across the bodies of the thirty-three young men, covered with wounds, lying in the green grass. They were all dressed the same, in a blue blouse decorated with the French national cockerel. One of the dead still had his fist in the air; next to him lay a man whose skull had been split open. The brains of another soldier lay scattered all over the ground, while a fourth soldier had been riddled with bullet holes, an absolutely appalling sight. There were no German dead or wounded; the French had been massacred and had not stood a chance against the well-trained troops. A doctor told me that they were part of the Garde Mobile and had been on their way to MacMahon's Army of Châlons but had been surprised by the

Prussians and were absolutely horrified to find out that the Germans had moved towards Châlons so quickly.

Although they were wearing blue blouses, the French cockerel and carrying the Chassepot rifle, it was very hard for us to treat them as franc-tireurs [men not fighting under military discipline and therefore regarded as guerrilla fighters] or prisoners of war. After today, the pretty countryside has lost its innocence forever and we realize that the enemy is everywhere.

On Saturday 27 and Sunday 28 August, the advance of the French Army was negligible. To be fair, torrential rain did not help matters. By nightfall I and XII Corps had reached the village of Le Chesne and V and VII Corps were at the village of Buzancy, where they had bumped into a party of Saxon cavalry. A short skirmish followed, resulting in the retreat of the Saxon vanguard. Again, the German army had moved much faster; they were only fifteen kilometres from Buzancy and Grandpré and, unbeknownst to the French, XII (Saxon) Corps was already in Stenay and approaching the river crossings of the River Meuse, the primary goal of the French V and VII Corps.

On 27 August, an unknown German eyewitness wrote in his diary:

'We are moving very fast; yesterday we were in Bar-le-Duc, now we are already in the Argonne. In spite of heavy rain and hail storms, the endless infantry and auxiliary columns have reached Clermont-en-Argonne. The small town that seems as if it is glued to the hill is almost exploding with German troops.'

Clermont-en-Argonne. According to a German eyewitness, 'the small town that seems as if it is glued to the hill is almost exploding with German troops'.

A mass grave in Varennes; ten Frenchmen and thirteen Germans were killed here during the course of a brief skirmish.

That same day, the leading Saxon Corps of the Army of the Meuse secured the river crossings of the Meuse at Dun-sur-Meuse and Stenay. They destroyed the bridges; the first available place for the French to cross the Meuse was now in Mouzon, fifteen kilometres north of Stenay.

On the night of Sunday 28 August, the Emperor and his entourage, who had travelled with I Corps, spent a comfortable night in a large house on the Main Street of Le Chesne. Little did they know that hostilities would start the next day and that the French army would be defeated just four days later. With the German Third Army sweeping northward on a broad front from Varennes to Vouziers and the Meuse Army already in place at Dun-sur-Meuse and Buzancy, MacMahon's army was marching deeper and deeper into Moltke's pocket.

Had Bazaine decided to and then succeeded in breaking through the encirclement of Metz, all kinds of new military possibilities would have opened up; if he had moved his force of 180,000 men north to attack the German armies from the rear or blocked their path of retreat at the Franco-German border, it would have caused major problems for Moltke. Instead, he and most of his generals chose to sit back and to wait for events to unfold.

CHAPTER 4

Nouart, Beaumont and Mouzon, 29-30 August

Monday 29 August: The skirmish at Nouart
On the evening of 28-29 August the tired French V and VII Corps halted at Dames Wood, part of a larger wooded area known as Belval Wood. Dames Wood is situated a few kilometres north of Nouart and Le Champy; from there, they were to march towards the river crossing at Stenay, some fifteen kilometres to the east.

On the afternoon of 28 August, an officer of VII Corps had spotted Prussian scouts. That night rifle shots were heard in the distance and the sky was lit up by a reddish glow. Convinced that they had been fired upon by armed civilians, the Prussians proceeded to set several villages ablaze. Vonq, Les Ailleux and Faillaise were systematically burnt to the ground and hundreds of people made homeless. The French army was nowhere to be seen, neither to defend the poor villagers nor to fight back.

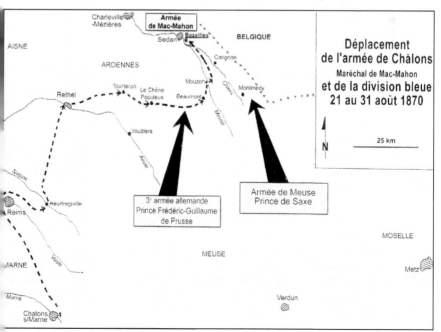

Marching routes of the Army of Châlons and the Prussian and Saxon armies.

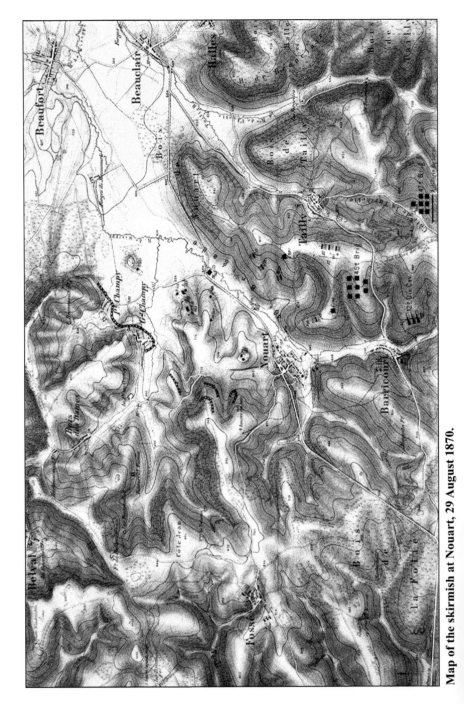

Map of the skirmish at Nouart, 29 August 1870.

General de Failly, commanding V Corps, was ordered to cross the River Meuse at Stenay as soon as possible. However, at nightfall on 28 August, Marshal MacMahon learned that the German XII Corps, under the command of Prince Georg von Sachsen, was already holding Stenay. Consequently, he decided that the following morning his whole Army would change direction and march north again in order to cross the River Meuse at Mouzon and Rémilly. As will be seen later, this would turn out to be a very dangerous decision as almost the whole of the Army of Châlons was now positioned in a very narrow corridor between Mouzon and Sedan, with the Germans approaching from the east, south and west. Sedan lies only eight kilometres from the Belgian border and, unless the French could cross the river and force a breakthrough in the south east, they would be trapped.

Luckily for the French the morning of Monday 29 August dawned bright and sunny; due to the incessant rain the day before they had spent a cold, wet, miserable night in Dames Wood. The French I and XII Corps, commanded by Generals Ducrot and Lebrun respectively, Napoleon III and the cavalry divisions of General Marguerite had all taken a more northerly route and were making good progress towards Mouzon and Rémilly. By noon, Lebrun's XII Corps, under MacMahon's supervision, had crossed the bridge at Mouzon; I Corps was close to the crossing at Rémilly and expected to continue east in the direction of Carignan.

The night before, however, Lieutenant Georges de Grouchy, after delivering MacMahon's new orders to General Douay, lost his way and rode his horse straight into a German cavalry patrol; the orders from MacMahon to be delivered to General de Failly were captured. Once again Moltke was fully aware of the whereabouts of the French and what they planned to do and so he adjusted his tactics accordingly; he ordered the Prussian Third Army to move to Beaumont in order to crush MacMahon's army before it could cross the Meuse. However, Moltke did not know that MacMahon's army had split up.

As a result, VII Corps, who had continued marching north to Mouzon and the V Corps, who had gone east, walked straight into the arms of the Germans who had been waiting for them at Stenay and in doing so divided MacMahon's southern wing of the Army of Châlons. Around noon, while French vanguards were crossing the marshy valley of the Wiseppe Creek, a tributary of the River Meuse, Failly's V Corps crashed into the vanguards of the 24th Saxon Division of XII Corps, commanded by Crown Prince Albert of Saxony. The German gunners reacted quickly; soon shells were exploding everywhere. Uncertain about the strength of the Germans, Failly's Corps retreated in the direction of Nouart and from the heights of Nouart Wood and Dames Wood their artillery started to

Nouart 2019. Apart from the ornamental fence, there is no trace of the 1870 burials.

return fire. The French infantry that thought they were heading for safety in Nouart were welcomed by rifle and gunfire; the village was already occupied by the 103rd Saxon Regiment. Hand-to-hand fighting ensued, but after a while the Germans and French both retreated, each uncertain of each other's strength.

This skirmish between the German and French armies, the first since the encirclement of Metz, resulted in 290 French and 363 German dead and wounded. Soon after the battle the bodies were looted by civilians and German soldiers and later buried in mass graves. Some soldiers were buried in Nouart Communal Cemetery; but, as far as is known, none of these graves remain today and the location of the mass grave(s) is lost.

Failly finally received his new orders late in the afternoon; his tired troops retreated under cover of darkness in the direction of the village of Beaumont, some twelve kilometres north-east of Nouart. At daybreak, after an exhausting night march through a forested area, the last units, more dead than alive, arrived at the fields near the village of Beaumont. By this time Failly's men were a disorganized mob that no longer obeyed orders; the 17,000 exhausted, hungry and disorganized men fell asleep where they were standing. No sentries had been positioned around the perimeter of the camp, a mistake that would cost them dearly the following day.

That night, in Château Grandpré, just twenty-five kilometres from Beaumont, King Wilhelm I of Prussia and his general staff went to their beds with the feeling that victory was within their grasp.

Château Grandpré in 2019.

Tuesday 30 August: The Battle of Beaumont.

In the early morning of Tuesday 30 August MacMahon paid a visit to Beaumont. He was hoping that Failly would be able to provide him with some information about the strength of the approaching German army. He could not. Failly accepted his new orders 'to cross the Meuse as soon as possible'. In effect this meant that he had to wake up his men who had just fallen asleep to tell them that they had to leave immediately; there was not even time for a proper breakfast. The men had not had anything to eat since the morning before and the combined hardships of hunger, fatigue and the terrible weather made them reluctant to obey orders. After MacMahon had left, Failly decided to wait for the supply trains; his men needed food, time to reorganize and to be properly resupplied with

The head of a German pickaxe, dated 1870, found in Nouart in 2019.

61

ammunition. The Marshal's advice to him was ignored, as well as information given by several worried farmers who had come to inform the general about the whereabouts of the approaching Germans.

By 11.30 am that day the rations had arrived and Failly's depleted Corps was busy cooking their meal; tents were pitched, rifles stacked and uniform coats were hung out to dry. The general himself, as well as most of his fellow officers, were enjoying a sumptuous meal in Beaumont, totally ignorant of the danger they were in. It was the calm before the storm.

The German reaction.

Château Grandpré had been a hive of activity the night before; new orders had been issued and numerous runners were coming and going. Since Moltke knew that the French army was looking for a way to cross the Meuse he wanted to attack them while they were still on the left bank. This was the moment when it was at its most vulnerable as its supply chain, soldiers and cavalry were all massing together in order to cross the few bridges in the area. Therefore Moltke and King Wilhelm decided to concentrate their forces in the Beaumont-Mouzon area; after the skirmish in Nouart and the capture of Lieutenant de Grouchy, they knew that the French V and VII Corps were heading for the bridge at Mouzon. Ready to strike, Moltke deployed his troops as follows:

Third Army:
V Corps, General von Kirchbach, 20,000 men and I Bavarian Corps, General von der Tann, 25,000 men. They were to advance towards Le Chesne; the 6th Bavarian Cavalry Division was already there observing French troop movements. In their attack on Beaumont the Bavarian Corps was also to support the left flank of the Fourth Army. The Third Army was ordered to attack the French from the rear and to pursue the French I Corps and VII Corps.

Fourth Army:
IV Corps, General Gustav von Alvensleben, 27,000 men, and XII Corps, Crown Prince Georg Von Sachsen, 30,000 men. Many soldiers and officers of XII Corps were from Magdeburg, capital of the Prussian province of Sachsen. Fourth Army was to advance north, directly to Beaumont, and go in pursuit of the French V and XII Corps.

Battle of Beaumont, 30 August 1870.

63

The confrontation.

As the men in Failly's army were just waking up, German scouts spotted them and immediately returned to their officers and reported what they had seen. It was decided to move the artillery into position in the forests and on to the ridges that surrounded the French camp, thus forming a semi-circle. As quietly as possible, the 8th Saxon Division, commanded by General von Schöler, took up position at the edge of Pont Gerache Wood. The heights a little north of Belle Voleé Farm and Beauséjour Farm were also occupied, almost in full view of the French encampment. Finally, at 12.30 pm, as many other German units were busy getting into position, someone in the French camp finally sounded the alarm.

General von Alvensleben wasted no time and immediately ordered the attack; in spite of the alarm almost all of Failly's V Corps was caught off guard. Many men had just woken up, others were having breakfast, fires were burning, the horses were being fed; the morning rituals of a waking army. It was total chaos when the bombardment of the camp started; shells exploded amongst men, tents and horses. Most of the German guns were positioned only 600 - 800 metres away from their targets and were lined up at the edge of the forest that surrounded the camp. Within seconds of the first barrage, the shouts and cries of the wounded and dying joined the thunder of the exploding grenades. Many panic-stricken men fled in disorder in the direction of Mouzon, with total disregard for fellow combatants and officers. However, German eyewitnesses reported that, in spite of the surprise attack, many of the French soldiers who were sitting closest to the Germans immediately formed a skirmish line that prevented the German infantry from taking the camp by storm. After the initial shock French officers tried to organize their men; several gunners manned their guns and the Reffye machine-guns. Some French units even tried to charge the heights near Belle Voleé Farm and Beauséjour Farm. This attempted attack soon petered out in the wake of withering rifle fire from the Saxon 16th Brigade (86th and 96th Regiments), who occupied the ridge, the aforementioned farms and Maison Blanche and Tuillerie Farms in order to protect their artillery against the attacking French. Soon, the Saxon 15th Brigade (31st and 71st Regiments) were called up to reinforce the 16th Brigade.

Meanwhile, on the right side of the French camp, the Saxon 13th Brigade of the 7th Division (26th and 66th Regiments) were also protecting gun batteries while the 14th Brigade (93rd and 27th Regiments) was heavily engaged on the Beaumont-Beaufort Road.

On the far left the soldiers of the Bavarian 2nd Division launched several charges from the forest, but were scattered in all directions by the rapid fire the French laid down with their superior Chassepot rifles. The

A French camp in peace time.

Reffye machine guns also played a key role in fending off the Germans; at such a close distance it proved to be a formidable weapon. However, the Germans managed to deploy more and more heavy guns and were wreaking havoc amongst the French ranks. The Bavarian infantry took heavy losses but continued to keep the pressure on the French; the Germans believed that speed of action and surprise were their best weapons.

By 1.15 pm, the German command, which had been hoping for an easy victory, were by now spurred to take more decisive action because of the stubborn resistance that the French were putting up and decided to charge the camp from three sides, supported by a heavy artillery barrage. The French were

A Magdeburger officer.

slowly forced to evacuate the camp; in some places fierce hand-to-hand fighting ensued but the majority of the French casualties were caused by murderous and accurate artillery fire. By approximately 2.00 pm the camp had ceased to be. The French had also been pushed out of Beaumont and were in full retreat to Mouzon. Many high ranking French officers, General Failly included, had managed to escape the fight unscathed. In fact, the French V Corps had largely escaped

65

annihilation only because of the initiative and resolute actions displayed by non-commissioned officers and their troops. Fortunately for the French, the road from Beaumont to Mouzon climbed steeply and the French guns and mitrailleuses placed here halted the German pursuit long enough for most of Failly's V Corps to reach the Meuse. While all hell was breaking loose at Beaumont, General Douay had left his headquarters in Stonne. However, the German V Corps were on his heels so quickly that they were almost breathing down his neck. Douay wanted to cross the Meuse at Mouzon as quickly as possible and continue to Carignan. However, while standing on a hill he heard the explosions and saw the pillars of smoke coming from the direction of Beaumont and hesitated. In his excellent book *Sedan 1870, The Eclipse of France*, Douglas Fermer describes Douay's decision: *In contrast to German commanders, who marched automatically to gunfire, Douay resolved to continue his march north-eastwards. Douay later claimed that he had been too far away to help V Corps, adding that no change of orders came from MacMahon. In any event, he marched away from Failly.*

While Douay was changing direction to continue his march to the north, away from Beaumont, part of his supply train, unaware of Douay's orders as no one had bothered to tell them, marched right into the arms of General von der Tann's Bavarians. Consequently it was practically destroyed while Douay and the remains of his army bravely scarpered north in the direction of Rémilly in order to cross the river there.

A few days after the battle, an article in the *Allgemeine Zeitung,* written by Felix Dahn, was published:

'When we entered the street that leads into the centre of Beaumont, we noticed that the town itself showed very little damage of the fighting. We later learnt that the French had first fought on the heights around Beaumont and later in the valley. However, the town centre and the church were swarming with French prisoners of war. Most of the houses had been commandeered and were now in use as first aid stations to take care of the wounded; German and French doctors and many volunteers were working frantically. The chaos in the town centre was so overwhelming that I hurried along the packed and narrow streets and made my way to the valley where the French camp had been raided. Just outside the little town, on the left side of the road near a large stone bridge, there were 900 French prisoners. Among them was a priest who had been caught firing at the Germans; he was to be executed in the next hour or so.

I continued in the direction of the battlefield when all of a sudden I found myself just a few feet away from the first dead; stretcher bearers and many other people were also there. The first man I saw was a French captain who had been shot through the head. He was lying face down over a ledge and was completely ransacked; all his pockets and bags were open and personal belongings without value for the looters were scattered all around him. I learnt that as soon as night falls over the battlefield the looting of the dead starts. It appears that it does not matter how many men of the military police are present, this horrific kind of behaviour seems unstoppable and thousands of ordinary soldiers are guilty of this despicable behaviour.

The sight of the rows of tents, partly collapsed, burnt or stampeded, showed me how surprised the French must have been by our attack; everything an army needed was lying scattered around just everywhere. While trying to save their lives they left everything behind as our bombardment must have taken them completely by surprise. At several places the Chassepot rifles were still standing upright, leaning against each other, and countless horses were killed still fixed to their pickets. There were dead soldiers still sitting around a smouldering fire, killed by shell splinters in their breast and with their plates and salt and pepper at the ready for lunch. Around 300 French were not yet buried; the rest of the dead had already been buried in mass graves.

Our soldiers were mainly killed by rapid fire from the excellent Chassepot rifle; many were shot through the head from a distance of about 350 metres. Most of the French on the other hand were killed by shellfire. The doctors found no bayonet or sabre wounds. The saddest thing to see are the many letters, written by mothers, wives, girlfriends and other relatives, thrown away by the pillagers, blowing across the fields.

The effects of shellfire were absolutely horrific. We found two groups of French soldiers, one group of five, the other of six, who were killed by the same shell; the first group, apparently, was just busy eating soup. The projectile had exploded at waist height; all the men were charred from knee to waist and the rest of their bodies were burnt just like their uniforms. There were also men among them whose skull or face had been blown off. One man had been decapitated by a shell splinter, but was still holding up his cup close to where his mouth used to be, ready to take a sip of his coffee.'

Retreat to Mouzon, 30 August 1870.

The Meuse Crossing at Mouzon

At Beaumont, the pathetic remains of what had once been General Failly's proud V Corps were on the run. In order to slow down the Germans and give the remainder of the Corps time to travel the eight kilometres to Mouzon, the retreating army mounted continuous rear guard actions on every hill and copse. The fighting continued for most of the afternoon. By about 5.00 pm the French were defending Mont de Brune, the last high ground south of Mouzon, but were eventually driven off the

68

Looking west from the outskirts of Mouzon to Mont de Brune.

hill. A French cavalry charge followed in order to keep the route to the bridge in Mouzon open, but all to no avail. They were ruthlessly punished by German artillery fire.

In spite of everything, many of the French managed to cross the bridge to escape being slaughtered in the narrow streets of Mouzon. This was partly because the Germans were being harassed by artillery fire from the east bank of the River Meuse. General Lebrun, who had managed to get his XII Corps across the river the day before, had come to Failly's aid. Lebrun had shouldered the responsibility and acted on his own initiative. This, as well as the dogged fight Failly's soldiers put up during their retreat, saved many French lives.

However, before the last Frenchman had been able to escape, fierce fighting had broken out in the town centre. By nightfall many houses were on fire, shells were exploding randomly and heavy hand-to-hand fighting ensued. Now it was a case of fighting for every street, every house; bodies were lying everywhere. To prevent the Germans from pursuing them, the infamous Reffye machine guns kept the bridge under continuous fire. The night remained disturbed by gunfire as stragglers desperately tried to find some way to cross the Meuse. Large numbers of French soldiers hid among the ruins of Beaumont and Mouzon and in the surrounding forests; skirmishes continued all night.

Felix Dahn reported:

'When the evening started to fall we packed up our things and started for the village of Mouzon. The wide country road that ran over the hills was littered with the remnants of war; besides the usual stuff like backpacks and rifles, it was covered with

69

The Reffye model 1866 machine gun, its twenty-five barrels clearly visible.

thousands of square wooden boxes, like cigar boxes, that contained twenty-five rounds for the French machine guns. Fortunately, these magazines are not going to be used against the German army any longer; we have learnt to respect these murderous weapons. Since the start of the war they have helped the French infantry and artillery gain a lot of time in order to retreat, while our infantry was forced to remain at a certain distance. All of a sudden, while we continued along the dark road in the direction of Mouzon, we came across a column of eleven guns. They had been captured from the French a few hours earlier.

I will never forget the sight that greeted my eyes when I entered the town – a train, chock-a-block with French prisoners, was ready to leave the station and everywhere in the town I could see dead bodies, French and German, smeared in blood, lying in the streets. Houses that had been taken by storm by the Prussians in the late afternoon, were in a sorry state, with broken windows and doors that had been smashed in with rifle butts; some houses had been burnt down and some had holes in the walls or roof which had been caused by the heavy artillery. The many bullet holes in the walls bore witness to the heavy fighting that had taken place in the streets. Several buildings were still on fire, casting an eerie glow across the town.

I looked to the left and saw the Meuse River. But what a sight! The retreating French had been massing at the bridge trying to get as much equipment, guns, ammunition etc. across as possible, when suddenly the German artillery opened fire. Grenades exploded amidst the French masses and now literally piles of dead soldiers, gun limbers and horses were all lying in the canal, an incredible sight, there was stuff strewn everywhere.

A 25 shot Reffye magazine. (Coll. Museé de la Dernière Cartouche)

Later, I met a Prussian officer with a wounded arm who told me that we should not enter the houses unarmed; there were still many Frenchmen hiding all over the place. Just as he finished talking, five Frenchmen, escorted by Prussian soldiers, were marched off in the direction of the railway station; they had just been caught hiding in a cellar somewhere. Another officer told us to go towards Sedan, so we jumped on a wagon, it was in the first column of wagons that was going in that direction. Through the darkness we could still see discarded equipment everywhere.

In order to avoid being caught in the German pincer, MacMahon ordered Failly (V Corps) and Douay (VII Corps) to withdraw to Sedan for temporary refuge. After travelling most of the night of 30-31 August, they finally reached the outskirts of Sedan, a small city of about 15,000 people. One cannot imagine the chaos that ensued when tens of thousands of hungry, demoralized, disorganized and panic-stricken soldiers thronged the narrow streets in search of food, drink and women.

By late in the afternoon Douay's VII Corps had managed to reach Rémilly, about four kilometres south of Sedan. Here they were to cross a pontoon bridge that had been built by the engineers. With the Germans hot on their trail, Douay did not want any delay in crossing the bridge but was in for a shock; Ducrot's I Corps was busy crossing the bridge and General de Bonnemain's 2nd Reserve Cavalry Division was awaiting its turn.

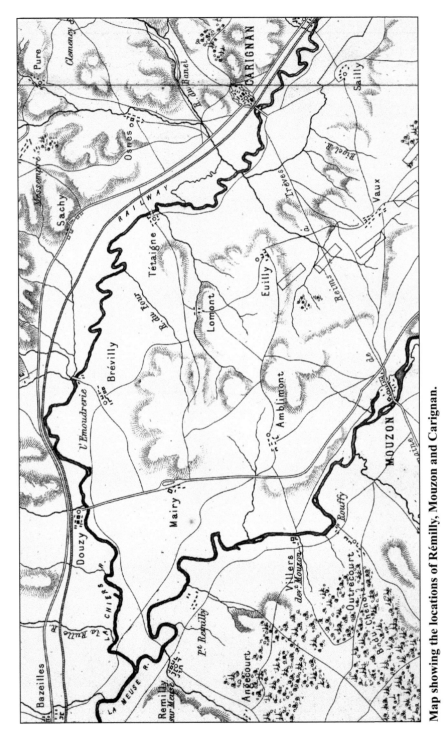

Map showing the locations of Rémilly, Mouzon and Carignan.

The Meuse Valley, showing Mouzon in the distance, ca 1870.

Ducrot's leading troops, who had been joined by the Emperor, were making good progress and were already approaching Carignan, some seventeen kilometres east of Rémilly. Finally, at around 10.00 pm, Douay's men started to cross with the aid of a fire at both ends of the pontoon bridge; it took more than four hours to get everybody to the other side. At around 2.00 am on the morning of 31 August, Major de Bastard of MacMahon's staff arrived with orders to stop marching east to Carignan/Montmédy and to march to Sedan instead, where the first troops – beaten in earlier fighting – had already started to arrive at around 5.00 am.

Totally ignorant of the events of the day, Napoleon, who was dining with his seventy strong entourage in Carignan, was absolutely flabbergasted when MacMahon's orders arrived. He had to catch the train to Sedan as soon as possible as the French on the right bank were in danger of being cut off by the Germans. Part of General Ducrot's I Corps, which had reached Carignan while on its way to Montmédy, was already retreating to Sedan.

Carignan was the closest the French ever got to Montmédy; they were forced to retreat just twenty-three kilometres short of their target. Bazeine, for his part, had not stuck to his side of the plan; he and his army were still trapped in Metz.

Conclusion.

The losses of 30 August had been appalling. It has been estimated that the French Army lost 7,500 men, of whom 5,700 were killed. The French had also lost huge quantities of irreplaceable material; in fact, there was not much left of fighting quality in V Corps. Of the 17,000 soldiers Failly had started out with, a mere 9,000 tired, hungry, disorganized and discouraged men had managed to reach the east bank of the Meuse and

An engraving of the church in Mouzon in use as a hospital. In reality there were hundreds of wounded cared for within its walls – the scene would have been far more chaotic.

had now joined Lebrun's XII Corps on their way to Sedan. In fact, all of MacMahon's army was now in retreat on Sedan. With the benefit of hindsight, the whole plan of breaking the Siege of Metz was doomed to disaster. Outmanoeuvred from the start, MacMahon never really stood a chance. The French had also lost 1,800 prisoners, twenty-eight cannon and eight mitrailleuses. In addition to this, V Corps lost its entire ammunition column of sixty wagons; they were left in orderly rows in Beaumont, as the drivers had fled with the horses.

The German losses were estimated at some 3,400 men. Amongst the German wounded was the commander of 16th Brigade, Colonel von Scheffler, and Colonel von Horn and Lieutenant Colonel von Hasse, both of the Saxon 86th Regiment. The Germans, however, had missed the opportunity of destroying half of MacMahon's Army of Châlons in Beaumont and Mouzay; if they had moved faster and been more determined, they could have cut off and encircled Douay's VII Corps at the same time as the attack on Beaumont had started. They had had all the advantages on their side: speed, intelligence, numerical superiority – they outnumbered the French two to one, but still the High Command was reluctant to deal the killer blow. In the end they were not able to prevent the French from crossing the Meuse.

CHAPTER 5

Bazeilles, 31 August-1 September

As the French were withdrawing to Sedan, Moltke issued new orders; like the rest of the German High Command, he sensed that the Germans were very close to victory. The French army, concentrated in and around Sedan, had its backs to the Belgian border; all Moltke and his army had to do was to close the circle. Therefore, he ordered the Third Army's V and XI Corps (100,000 men), Crown Prince Friedrich Wilhelm of Prussia, to move forward speedily along the left bank of the River Meuse to Donchery/Sedan and to secure the river crossings in order to cut off a possible French retreat to the west, ie the Charleville-Mézières-Paris railheads. The Fourth Army (of 150,000 men), Crown Prince Albert of Saxony, was to march along the right bank of the River Meuse to Sedan, with its right wing extended to the Belgian border. Moltke's orders aimed to compress the French 'into the smallest possible space between that river [Meuse] and the Belgian frontier'.

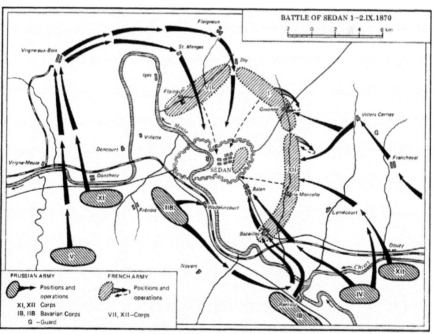

After the French retreated across the Meuse to Bazeilles and Sedan, the German Armies immediately started the encirclement.

On the afternoon of Wednesday 31 August, spearheads of General von der Tann's 1st Bavarian Corps, closing in on Sedan from the left bank of the River Meuse, discovered that the railway bridge at Bazeilles was still intact. Spotting the danger, the French sent a demolition party to destroy the bridge. Before the French could finish their work, a company of Bavarian troops under Captain Slevogt crossed the bridge, after which chaotic fighting broke out. In the end the French were forced to retreat. Quickly, the Bavarians discarded the barrels of gunpowder and started chasing the French across a meadow that lies between the bridge and the village of Bazeilles. More troops followed and soon a whole battalion, about 500 men, entered the town.

However, that morning, at around 7.00 am, the 'Blue Division', the 1st and 2nd Marine Brigades under General Vassoigne, took up billets just a little north of Bazeilles. Alarmed by rifle fire, they quickly went into action and once again a fight broke out. The French commander ordered his men to fix bayonets (*Á la fourchette!*) and slowly the Bavarians were pushed back to the southern part of the town. Von der Tann ordered reinforcements to cross the bridge and instructed his artillery to open fire. Soon shells were raining down on the streets, setting fire to several buildings. In the meantime, the French had put some of their feared mitrailleuses in position and started to pour a withering fire into the German troops. By 3.15 pm, it was all over; the Germans had taken a severe beating and under cover of a heavy artillery barrage, to prevent the French following on their tails, they retreated back to the railway bridge; this remained under Bavarian control. At the end of this impromptu battle, the French had lost 400 men, the Germans 142, including Captain Slevogt, and several houses in Bazeilles were ablaze. Von der Tann suspended all further operations and awaited reinforcements; the Fourth Army, approaching on the right bank, was on its way.

That night, Moltke, who had moved his headquarters to Château Hannonet in Vendresse, decided that the offensive would be renewed at 5.00 am. The encirclement of Sedan was almost complete, the railway line to Charleville-Mézières had been cut and the Meuse crossings, most notably the one at Donchery, were safely in German hands. By this time the situation for the French had become dire; 110,000 soldiers were trapped in and around Sedan and were facing a force three times the size of their own. Fortunately, there was ammunition in abundance, but, on the downside, only enough rations to feed the army for two days. On the afternoon of 31 August, General Failly of V Corps, who had performed extremely badly since the start of the campaign, was replaced by General de Wimpffen, who had a letter from the Minister of Defence, Palikao,

The railway bridge near Bazeilles.

authorizing him to take over command should the Army of Châlons need to be led by a stronger hand. Wimpffen, an ambitious man, and MacMahon were not the best of friends. In Sedan, Wimpffen took his orders from an exhausted MacMahon, but did not tell him about the letter. By telegraphing Palikao that the withdrawal to Sedan was only a temporary measure to gain time to reorganize and re-equip his forces, MacMahon again avoided making a decision about how to continue the war from this dire situation.

General v. Wimpffen.

General de Wimpffen, 1811-1884.

General Vassoigne, occupied with matters elsewhere, appointed Captain Arsène Lambert as commander of a small detachment of marines to guard the town and to prevent the Germans continuing their advance on Sedan. During the night of 31 August/1 September, Captain Lambert and his marines had not been sitting idle; while the Bavarians were (presumably) sleeping, they had been busy building barricades on the main road

Captain Arsène Lambert, 1834-1901.

leading into Sedan and had occupied several places, among them several sturdy and fortified buildings along the main street. The gleam of the burning houses made it possible to work well into the night; by 1.00 am the tired men were still working, assisted by armed civilians. Lambert and his troops were preparing a warm welcome for the Bavarians. The French finally put up a fight: but it was too little and too late.

At about 4.00 am on the morning of Thursday 1 September, the first two columns of Bavarian troops, hoping to take Bazeilles by surprise, started crossing the railway and pontoon bridges on the Meuse. It was extremely foggy and they managed to cross the field between the bridge and the town unseen. Arriving at the outskirts of the town, the column started in a northern direction along the main street in Bazeilles. Seeing the deserted streets, they thought they had outsmarted the French and some of the Bavarians started to cheer. However, a few moments later, at approximately 4.15 am, the first salvo of French Chassepot rifles ripped through the silence of the night. The Germans reacted promptly, but were completely surprised and fierce fighting broke out. As time progressed both German and French commanders threw more and more troops into the fray and soon the whole of the town was an orgy of death and violence. At daybreak big columns of smoke could be seen above the town due to the burning buildings; the smell of gunpowder filled the air. In the narrow streets there were scenes of fierce close-quarter combat; soldiers were pursuing one another through gardens, houses and cellars, with civilians and livestock fleeing in every direction. However, not all of the civilians acted as passive spectators; there are several reports of armed townspeople firing at and killing Germans. When the Germans caught them they were executed on the spot.

As the streets were under constant gunfire, many people, soldiers and civilians alike, perished in the burning and collapsing buildings. It was a brutal struggle where no quarter was given on either side. Once again the Bavarians were pushed back to the southern part of the town but, despite the French machine guns, somehow managed to hold on to it. Villa Beurmann, changed into a fortress by the French, was a key position in preventing the Germans from reaching Sedan. Von der Tann now decided to launch several attacks to try to outflank the French marines and to force a breakthrough at that point. In doing so he also hoped to establish contact with units of the Fourth Army to force the French out of the gardens of Château Monvillers, not far from Villa Beurmann. In the savage fighting that broke out, the French managed to keep the château gardens and the villa under their control.

However, by now the German Fourth Army had by-passed Bazeilles to the north-east, and was trying to get a footing in the village of La

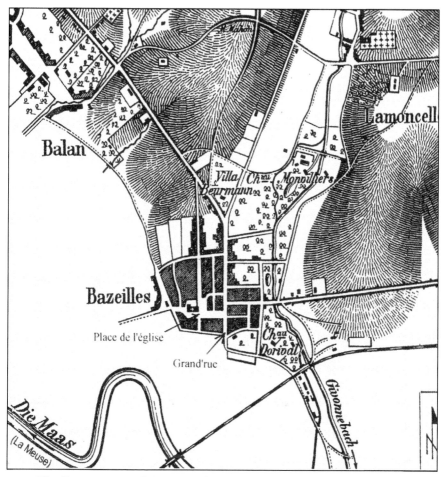

The Germans started the attack from the railway. The final fighting took place in the white rectangular areas to the left of Villa Beurmann.

Moncelle, some two kilometres to the north. They were greeted by withering Chassepot rifle fire and it took the Saxon gunners two hours before they finally had their guns in position; they had suffered terrible losses. By now, the fighting that was raging from Bazeilles to Daigny, a hamlet a little north of La Moncelle and where the French had managed to keep control over the bridge across the Givonne River, had become a stalemate.

Nevertheless, the Germans deployed more troops and significant numbers of the superior Krupp guns were brought into action. Slowly but surely, the pressure on the French increased as did the number of their casualties.

79

Prussian gunners.

MacMahon out of action.

At 5.45 am, learning about the fierce fighting that was going on in Bazeilles, MacMahon mounted his horse and rode from Sedan to the heights of La Moncelle to assess the situation himself. Suddenly, a nearby exploding shell broke his horse's leg and wounded MacMahon in the buttock; when he tried to dismount he lost consciousness. When he came to (briefly), he ordered General Ducrot to take over command, unaware of de Wimpffen's secret orders. (See the map at the beginning of this chapter, p.74; MacMahon was wounded along the road from Balan to La Moncelle.)

At about 7.30 am, amidst the chaos of the battlefield, General Ducrot learnt that he was in charge of the Army of Châlons; he immediately ordered the army to retreat to the heights of Illy as he believed this to be a much easier place to defend than the Sedan trap. In fact, General Ducrot had never agreed with MacMahon's plan of taking up position in Sedan as made clear in his legendary remark, *We are in a chamber pot and we're going to be shat on*. At 9.00 am, he gave the orders for the evacuation of Bazeilles. However, some time later, a startled Ducrot was informed by General de Wimpffen about his authority. De Wimpffen immediately issued counter orders; there would be no retreat and he ordered Ducrot to resume the attack. By 10.00 am, Saxon troops had managed to push the French out of Daigny and had taken possession of the village; the French 3rd Zouaves, forced to retreat, had fled in disarray, abandoning their guns and machine guns. With the French out of the way, the Saxons

The MacMahon Cross marks the spot where the general was hit by shrapnel.

renewed their attack on La Moncelle and also on the gardens at Château Monvilliers. From here, the Saxons fought their way to Villa Beurmann, which was still holding out against all odds, buying the slowly retreating French marines valuable time. Attacked from three sides, the situation became untenable and the exhausted garrison was forced to leave the premises after almost seven hours of fighting. An anonymous French soldier described the scene:

A Bavarian six pounder crew.

'The enemy infantry came straight for us and from three directions; we could only fend them off with enormous efforts. As soon as they showed their heads above a wall or loophole we fired at them or stabbed them with our bayonets. The Germans were like ants; as soon as one was neutralized, another one clambered over the dead body of his predecessor, yelling and screaming all the time, trying to intimidate us. We also screamed at the top of our lungs, and this, combined with the sound of bullets whizzing by, the clatter of swords and bayonets, the gurgling of the dying, the crackling of the rifles, exploding shells, collapsing walls, breaking glass and the air thick with gunpowder defies every imagination. The battle became more and more savage and chaotic.'

At around the same time, General Vassoigne received Ducrot's orders to retreat; he ordered his troops to withdraw to Balan, about two kilometres north-west of Bazeilles. Meanwhile, isolated pockets of French marines continued to fight against the Bavarians in Bazeilles; little remained of the town itself, which by now had been almost razed to the ground. A little later Vassoigne received De Wimpffen's orders to halt the retreat and to retake what was left of the town; but by now it was impossible to return to the blazing town as the Germans were already advancing on Balan and were pouring a deluge of shell-fire into the French columns trying to reach Bazeilles. To be fair to all involved it was a miracle that *any* orders came through; communications were a shambles during the whole Sedan campaign.

Last stand at the Taverne Bourgerie.

The isolated marines in Bazeilles determined to continue fighting, hoping that some of them could escape to safer ground and resume the fight elsewhere. Slowly retreating to the north of the town, Captain Jean-Baptiste Bourgey and about fifty officers barricaded themselves into the last house in the village, the Taverne Bougerie, at the northern end of Bazeilles. Here they managed to withstand countless attacks, causing heavy casualties on the attacking Bavarians. After more than four hours

Artist's impression of the attack on Taverne Bourgerie.

The famous painting of Alphonse de Neuville: Captain Lambert firing the last round. Incredibly, most of the interior has been preserved.

of fighting the French started to run out of ammunition. Even worse for the small garrison was that the German artillery had joined the orgy of destruction. The French, with eighteen men wounded and out of ammunition, decided to surrender after Captain Georges Aubert fired the last cartridge at the Bavarian troops. After the white flag went up a German officer was barely able to prevent the Bavarian troops from massacring the surrendering Marines; later the French garrison were congratulated by a Bavarian divisional commander, who was extremely impressed by their resistance.

After the battle an anonymous eyewitness wrote that:

'[…] the dead and heavily wounded were thrown on piles together with body parts that were lying around everywhere, ripped off by shells. Some bodies were missing their heads, as if they were chopped off by a blunt axe; other ones were missing arms or legs or both. There was no time to extract the wounded from the piles of dead; they would suffocate slowly under the weight of the bodies lying on top of them. This sometimes took several days. Arms and legs were sticking out of the piles of yellowish white flesh; the smell was unbearable.'

At a substantial cost in human lives Bazeilles was laid totally waste. According to French and German sources, the French army suffered 2,655 casualties; the Bavarian Army lost 213 officers and 3,876 men. Although French propaganda told of massacres of men, women and children, an official French investigation found that, although the town had largely been destroyed, only forty-two civilians from Bazeilles had died. Among the dead were several people who had been executed by the Bavarians as franc-tireurs or partisans; in the following months, 150 more people died from injuries. The total number of casualties of the ten-hour battle in Bazeilles has been estimated at 6925.

Bazeilles had been a black day for the Bavarian army; at this stage of the

Bullets and shrapnel found on the battlefield. (Coll. Thibault Mansy)

84

The bombed and burned out Grande Rue (Main Street) in Bazeilles.

war they had not expected that the French would still be capable of putting up such fierce resistance. In France after the war the Battle of Bazeilles became the symbol of French resistance to the Prussians; in fact they felt that the battle at Bazeilles should somehow have saved what little honour, if any, that was left after the terrible defeat at Sedan. Therefore, it is not surprising that the only museum on the subject of the fiasco at Sedan, which is dedicated to the French marines, is located in Bazeilles.

With the loss of Bazeilles, La Moncelle and Daigny, the south-east route to Sedan was wide open. To the south-west the bridge at Donchery had already been taken by German troops, consequently cutting off the only route for a retreat to Charleville-Mézières. The Belgian border to the north did not help matters either; the French were almost surrounded on all sides and were in danger of being destroyed in the Sedan cauldron, a process that was already underway. Napoleon III and his brand-new army commander, General de Wimpffen, were facing an impossible situation.

CHAPTER 6

Sedan: 1 September

After spending a comfortable night in the village of Vendresse, staying in the homes of local nobility, Prussian King Wilhelm I (Château Hannonet), Bismarck (Villa La Roques) and the Prussian Crown Prince (Château de la Cassine in Cassine, a hamlet a little north of Vendresse) set off for Sedan. Together with their following and journalists of the international press, they took up position on the Colline de Frénois (Frénois Hill). On today's maps this position is marked as Tue Chevaux [Dead Horses], Hill 290.) From the high ground they had first class seats for the drama that was about to play out in the valley below: the encirclement of Sedan and the defeat of Napoleon's army. British journalist Edward Legge wrote in his memoir that,

> 'On the plateau, near the batteries (which, by the way, were never silent), I saw in the afternoon General Moltke, General von Avensleben, General Schöler, General the Prince of Rudolstadt and many other distinguished officers. The King and the Crown Prince were on the hills to the left, near the Meuse.'

At 10.00 am on Thursday 1 September 1870, the Army of Châlons started the battle with 202 infantry battalions, eighty cavalry squadrons and 564 guns, attacking the surrounding Prussian Third and Meuse Armies totalling 222 infantry battalions, 186 cavalry squadrons and 774 guns. General De Wimpffen, the new commander of the French V Corps and

SEDAN
BALAN
Frenois Hill

the Army of Châlons, hoped to launch a combined infantry and cavalry attack against the surrounding German forces in order to break out of the Sedan cauldron. However, by 11.00 am the loss of Bazeilles, La Moncelle and Daigny, ie the right flank of the Sedan defences, and the German occupation of the bridge across the Meuse at Donchery, immediately blocked De Wimpffen's orders to keep the passage to the bridge open. The noose around Sedan was tightening and the deadly accurate Prussian artillery fire became more and more powerful while French losses in men and materiel were rapidly mounting.

The right flank.

By now, the village of Givonne, a little north of Daigny and providing the last defences on Sedan's right flank, had become the focus of German attention. Although Givonne was quickly taken by the Bavarians and Saxons, at the hamlet of Haybes, situated in a ravine halfway between Daigny and Givonne, a fierce artillery duel broke out between the Guard Corps, under Prince August of Württemberg, and the gunners of Ducrot's I Corps. The French had placed their artillery on the western heights above Haybes, the Germans on the eastern heights, while the infantry fought below in the ravine where the hamlet was situated. It took the Germans until midday to dislodge the stubborn French defenders from the village.

The main priority of Crown Prince Albert of Saxony's Fourth Army was to achieve a breakthrough here and to continue westwards; his aim was to join up with the Third Army and complete the encirclement. The Germans managed to increase the pressure; Ducrot's I Corps started to lose cohesion and withdrew to Garenne Wood, north of Sedan, only to discover that these woods were within range of the powerful Krupp guns. With Lebrun's XII Corps retreating in the east, the perimeter around Sedan was reduced again.

BAZEILLES

BATAILLE DE SEDAN
Position des troupes Françaises
et Allemandes à 3 heures.

FRANÇAIS ▨▨▨ ALLEMANDS ▬▬

G   *Garde royale*
S   *Saxons*
I B *1er corps bavarois*
2 B *2me corps bavarois*
4   *IVe corps d'armée*
C.D. *Division de cavalerie*
W *Corps Wurtembergeois*
11 *XIe corps d'armée*
5   *Ve corps d'armée*
R   *Réserves de la 3me armée*
b   *Batteries*

The left flank.

Early on the morning of 1 September, Crown Prince Friedrich of Prussia ordered the V and XI Corps to complete the encirclement from the west. The army set off at around 8.00 am and reached St. Albert and St. Menges an hour later, without encountering much opposition. This action also meant that the village of Illy was now within reach of the German guns, thereby sealing off the last escape route to the west for Napoleon's right flank, Ducrot's I and Lebrun's XII Corps.

Exploiting their success, the Germans rushed to the village of Illy to the east to complete the encirclement, but this was still in French hands. In the meantime, several German companies had arrived in Floing, where they managed to hold out long enough until the artillery arrived. Their

88

goal was to reach the ridge that runs from Floing in roughly an east to west line. The so-called Floing Heights (or Le Terme Heights) were the last barrier between the German army and Sedan. It was on these heights that Douay's VII Corps had taken up position. An artillery duel started between a few German guns situated on the heights south of St. Menges (Hatois Hill) and eight batteries (thirty-two guns) of French smooth barrelled guns. At first the Germans took a severe beating but after the arrival of more of their gun batteries (a total of seventy-two guns) they gradually got the upper hand.

At 11.30 am, Wimpffen, thinking that this was not a serious attack, ordered Douay to send reinforcements to Lebrun on the right flank, thereby weakening his own position on the left. However, the French batteries on Floing Heights were still firing, the troops had prepared light field entrenchments and the machine guns inflicted heavy casualties amongst the German troops and gunners.

While the German infantry was deploying north-eastwards, the French cavalry thought it saw its chance. The regiments of the Chasseurs d'Afrique, under General Jean Auguste Marguerite (1823-1870), were to charge westwards to the village of Illy and continue to the German guns at St. Menges. The Germans watched them coming and opened fire at fifty metres, plastering the first regiment with shell and rifle fire. Having lost ninety-seven men, the regiment and its supporting two regiments hurried back to their starting point amidst the exploding shells. In the meantime, the French had launched an all-out attack to recapture Floing;

Marguerite's cavalry charge at Illy.

but it remained firmly in German hands. Around noon, the German Third and Fourth Armies managed to join up; the French were now completely surrounded, and droves of French soldiers who were just outside the encirclement, started for the Belgian border. Edward Legge reported:

> 'Our way was through fields covered with the dead and dying of both armies. Some were lying with their hands crossed on their breasts, their glassy eyes fixed upon the blue vault of Heaven; others lay, as they fell, in a heap; some had fallen into the ditches and streams that permeated the valley; a French chasseur, shot through the heart, was lying in a stream, his head resting on his knees, and his rifle still grasped firmly with both hands. A ghastly sight it was, and one that is printed indelibly on my memory. It was now noon, and the French were slowly retreating on Sedan. Nothing could resist the onward movement of German troops, who kept up a perpetual enfilade.'

In the meantime, the condition of the encircled soldiers in the Sedan cauldron was worse than ever; with the encirclement complete, the Germans started pounding Sedan and surroundings with their guns, comfortably positioned on the high ground. Down in the Sedan Cauldron morale faltered as thousands of French soldiers discarded their equipment

The Sedan defences, designed by the famous military engineer Vauban (1633-1707).

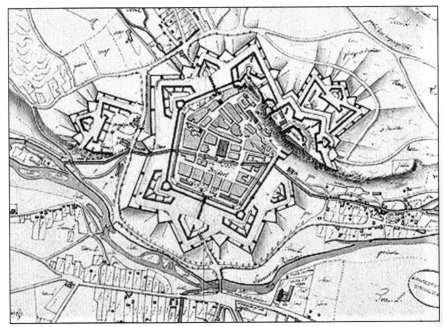

The Calvaire d'Illy today (2019) looking north, with Illy in the centre background.

and started to flee in all directions to escape the slaughter. Many made for the already overcrowded citadel; in several places unarmed French soldiers started to fistfight their way for shelter.

Trying desperately to defend the Plateau of the Calvaire d'Illy, the high crest between Floing Heights and Illy, officers tried to rally as many troops as possible. Under the direction of General Doutrelaine (1820-1881), the infantry tried to cling on to the crest despite the heavy bombardment. Artillery was called in but to no avail; the German gun fire was so overwhelming that many of the guns, gun crews and ammunition carts were destroyed before they could be put in position. The losses were staggering and by 2.00 pm the French had been driven off the hill by a devastating bombardment; in disarray they fled to Givonne Wood at the southern tip of Floing Heights. General Doutrelaine was taken prisoner. In spite of being chased by German infantry, the French somehow organized a counter-attack that drove the enemy out of the woods.

The French defences were now being pounded from all sides; all of the French corps were slowly but surely pushed back towards Sedan. Although the French gunners steadily returned fire, with every passing minute the situation in town was worsening, as witnessed by King Wilhelm and his retinue who, in spite of all the smoke and dust, had a relatively clear view of the battlefield from their elevated position on Frénois Hill.

German soldiers storming the Floing Heights, 1 September 1870.

The last French cavalry charge at Floing.

To the north of Sedan, the Germans, feeling that victory was within grasp, started simultaneously pushing up the slopes of Floing Heights and the Calvaire d'Illy. They were now within one kilometre of Sedan; the loss of the heights would mean the loss of the city. Something had to be done to stop the Germans from taking the ridge, so General Ducrot ordered Marguerite's cavalry to advance across Floing Heights, charge the Germans off the hill and retake Floing. With an avalanche of shells bursting all over the ridge, this was nothing less than a suicide mission.

Marguerite went forward to explore the terrain whilst his African Chasseurs prepared themselves for the attack. Ducrot had already left the site as he was hoping to find the necessary infantry to accompany the horsemen. Meanwhile Marguerite was hit by a bullet. It passed through his cheeks and smashed his jaw; severely wounded, he died five days later on 6 September in Maubeuge in Belgium. General Galliffet, quickly appointed to be Marguerite's successor, finally ordered the charge and the three regiments, some 1,800 men, started crossing Floing Heights and were met with a devastating bombardment. Men fell like dominoes and the chaos and the din of battle was indescribable. The French charged down the slopes and some even made it into Floing but the ridge quickly became strewn with dead soldiers and horses. In the chaos that followed the remaining Chasseurs retreated back to Garenne Wood, disregarding

The cavalry charge at Floing.

any obstacle in their way, causing mayham amongst Douay's infantry in the process. To add to the shambles, the French artillery opened fire on Marguerite's retreating cavalry, mistaking them for Germans.

Some historians consider that this was the last 'old school' cavalry charge in western Europe; it had lasted over half an hour and almost a 1,000 cavalrymen had laid down their lives. (Incredibly, and in spite of having studied the 1870 campaign in detail, the same mistake was made several times by cavalry charging (much improved) machine guns in the opening battles of 1914.)

As a result, French resistance collapsed, the heights were taken by the Germans and Ducrot's VII Corps fled to Sedan. Followed by frenzied German troops, the enemy stood before its walls by around 4.00 pm, only held in check by the fortress guns. The Germans started an unprecedented bombardment on Sedan and Garenne Wood, where thousands of soldiers had sought refuge. Some sources mention that between 1.00 pm to 4.00 pm over 600 guns fired more than 33,000 shells into the cauldron. From all sides, unarmed and panic-stricken soldiers were trying to make it for illusory safety behind the walls of Sedan.

Napoleon surrenders.

While in all sectors the French were retreating on Sedan, General de Wimpffen was planning an attack on Balan in a last-ditch effort to break out to Carignan: *rather than to be taken prisoner in the fortress of Sedan. Let Your Majesty come and place himself amid his troops [...].* Instead, Napoleon ordered the white flag to be raised over the Citadel as he was not willing to sacrifice further lives in a lost cause. The flag was not acknowledged by the Germans because de Wimpffen and approximately 6,000 men were still holding out and were desperately counter attacking the German troops at Balan. This only led to more casualties, as the

93

The front page of the *London Gazette* of 17 September 1871 symbolically shows Napoleon III waving a white flag.

French were pulverized by such unrelenting artillery fire that no building in Balan was left standing. This did not stop de Wimpffen from returning to Sedan to try to rally more troops; he managed to find 2,000 men and returned to the Balan butchery.

In the meantime, one by one, Napoleon's beaten generals arrived at the Sous Préfecture (sub-prefecture) in Sedan; by 4.00 pm, the war was in effect over. Sedan became almost overwhelmed by the thousands of stragglers that were wandering through the streets, while Louis Napoleon was conferring with his generals Douay, Ducrot and Lebrun, thereby annulling de Wimpffen's authority. It hardly mattered; Napoleon's army was on the brink of collapse. Only de Wimpffen and a few thousand men were still trying to break out of the encirclement. Amazingly, amidst the bursting shells, they succeeded in breaking out of Balan and managed to reach the northern outskirts of Bazeilles; it was the last spasm of a dying army. The German guns pounded de Wimpffen's troops so hard that whole companies were all but wiped out by the exploding shells, leaving no option but to retreat back to Sedan. Eventually the Emperor finally made a decisive decision: with no hope of breaking out and seeing everything around him being destroyed, Napoleon III called off the attacks and once again ordered the white flag to be raised; a note was sent to the Germans requesting an armistice. But de Wimpffen, completely out of touch with reality, refused to sign anything; instead, he continued the attack on Balan. By the end of the day, when he finally realized that all was lost, he ordered the retreat towards Sedan, to be lead by Lebrun, who had joined the fight during the afternoon. One by one, the German guns fell silent.

Not long after, Lieutenant Colonel Paul Bronsart von Schellendorff of von Moltke's staff entered Sedan under a white flag to demand capitulation. He returned to King Wilhelm with a sealed note that had been personally given to him by Napoleon. On his return, Wilhelm, Moltke and Bismarck were amazed to discover that Napoleon was still amongst his troops; they thought that he had fled to Paris long before the Siege of Sedan. Napoleon's note read: *Having failed to die amongst my troops, there is nothing left for me to do but to place my sword in the hands of Your Majesty. Napoleon.*

Lieutenant Colonel von Schellendorff, (1832-1891).

General Reille, who had accompanied von Schellendorff, returned to Sedan at about 7.00 pm with the following reply: *Regretting the circumstances in which we meet, I accept the sword of Your Majesty and appoint General Moltke [...] to negotiate the capitulation of the army that has fought so bravely under your orders. Wilhelm.*

That evening, armed with full powers to negotiate, de Wimpffen, accompanied by Chief of Staff General Faure, set off to Donchery, where Moltke was using the mayor's house as a headquarters; Bismarck and a number of high-ranking officers were also present. Moltke presented the terms of surrender: the entire French army would become prisoners of war; all equipment and arms would be confiscated; officers were allowed to keep their side arms. De Wimpffen refused to accept the deal; he would rather see his army leaving the battlefield with flying flags and honour. This, of course, was refused by von Moltke and both the French and Germans suggested resuming fighting. However, Bismarck suggested de Wimpffen return to his Emperor and talk things over; if not, hostilities would recommence at 9 o'clock the next morning.

Friday 2 September: Capitulation.

Unsatisfied with the outcome of the negotiations, Napoleon finally decided to take matters into his own hands. The ill-looking and fatigued Emperor reached Donchery at about 6.00 am but refused to enter the town; instead he suggested that negotiations take place in a weaver's house located on the main route from Sedan to Mezières, the present-day D764.

The first meeting between Bismarck (left) and Napoleon.

Sitting on simple wooden chairs outside the weaver's house, Napoleon tried to talk the Germans into more favourable, and more importantly, more honourable conditions of capitulation, but Bismarck and Moltke stuck to their guns. In the meantime, in Sedan, de Wimpffen and his generals had realized that it would be impossible to resume hostilities and therefore decided that it would be better to accept the German terms. Napoleon, however, declared himself a prisoner of war and shifted all the responsibility onto the Government in Paris, unaware that his high command had already accepted the terms.

Napoleon III and Bismarck sitting outside the weaver's home in Donchery.

As the outcome of the meeting at the weaver's house was unsatisfactory to both parties, a new meeting was planned at Château Bellevue, near Frénois. Here, in the presence of Napoleon and Bismarck, de Wimpffen and Moltke signed the military capitulation of Sedan and the Army of Châlons. After the signing, Prussian King Wilhelm came down from his headquarters on the hill in front of Marfée Wood to meet Napoleon. The two had a private conversation in which Wilhelm offered the fallen Emperor the castle of Wilhelmshöhe in Kassel (Hesse, Germany) for his internment; Napoleon accepted thankfully.

After Napoleon's surrender, an unknown officer of the British Royal Artillery observed the battlefield and wondered how it had been possible that the French had held out for as long as two days; he deemed the terrain totally unsuitable for defensive fighting.

'In many instances the German position, the high ground, commands the French position. However, the numerous dips and extensive forests in the latter offered facilities for massing under shelter large bodies in reserve. The striking feature of the site is of course Sedan itself, whose weak old-fashioned bastion trace, with its antiquated flimsy escarps and ramparts, must have been constructed on principles which never dreamed that the fortress could be attacked by any weapon more powerful than the old smooth bore 32 pounder. In fact, Sedan, the toe of the horseshoe,

97

is situated, as it were, at the bottom of a basin, with the ground sloping upwards from it on all sides.

A single glance suffices to show in what desperate straits MacMahon was placed. In the first instance, out-flanked, outnumbered and cramped into an insufficient space, he had no elbow-room to fight. If any portion of his line were forced, the rest of the position was, from its semicircular shape, at once bulged out and taken in the rear.

As the day wore on, the extreme flanks of the Prussians effected a junction near Givonne; the circle became more and more contracted until at last the disordered and despairing French were absolutely thrust down into the bottom of the funnel represented by Sedan. Then indeed they were at the mercy of their victors who, crowding their guns on the closely surrounding hilltops, from whence they could peer into the town, as good as said to its defenders, 'Surrender; else you and your puny defences will be swept off the face of the earth'. In fine, our original surprise at the French capitulation and wonder of their not having attempted, at all hazards, to cut their way out of the trap, is now changed into amazement, that, on awakening on the morning of 1 September, and finding themselves in such a desperate crisis, they could have summoned resolution enough to fight a battle at all, with the almost certainty of impending defeat; from the moment the first shot was fired, the result was a foregone conclusion.'

Casualties during the Battle of Sedan were calculated – though not necessarily conclusively: the Germans had lost 2,320 men killed, 5,910 wounded and 702 missing, a total of 8,932 casualties; the French had lost 3,000 dead, 14,000 wounded and 21,000 prisoners, a total of 38,000 casualties. In all, 120,000 French were removed from taking part in any further action in the war; the Army of Châlons had ceased to exist.

The small area where the fighting had taken place was littered with dead; there were corpses and dead horses lying everywhere; it was said that it was near impossible to visit the area on horseback as there was no space left on the ground for the horse's hooves. The beautiful summer weather resulted in high temperatures, making the clearing of the battlefield a horrendous job.

'Mass graves were dug, and sometimes a wounded man who was still alive was extracted from the piles of rotting flesh. The digging of the mass graves to bury the dead took several days. During the night human vultures came out to see if there were any valuables

Château Bellevue then

… and now.

on the bodies; clothes were stolen or cut to pieces with knives. All kinds of personal effects were littering the battlefields. These vultures were not only local people thinking that their ship had finally come in, but many opportunist soldiers were smashing in faces to get any gold teeth out.'

Today, thousands of German and French soldiers still lie in – mostly unmarked and unknown – mass graves in the area around Sedan.

CHAPTER 7

Aftermath

The defeat of the French at Sedan had decided the war in Prussia's favour; however, it would drag on for five more months. With Bazaine's army immobilized and besieged in the City of Metz, no other forces stood on French soil to prevent a German invasion and the capture of Paris. But things were not as easy as the Germans had hoped for.

Change of regime: the Government of National Defence. When news of the disaster at Sedan and Emperor Napoleon's capture reached Paris, the French Second Empire was immediately overthrown in a bloodless and successful coup d'état in Paris on Sunday 4 September, led by General Trochu, Jules Favre, and Léon Gambetta. They abolished the second Bonapartist monarchy and proclaimed a republic led by a Government of National Defence; the Third Republic.

French commemorative war medal.

Meanwhile, Napoleon III was taken to Germany and released several months later. Reunited with his wife Eugénie and his son Prince Eugène, he went into exile in the United Kingdom; Already a very sick man, Napoleon III died on 9 January 1873 in Chislehurst, Kent.

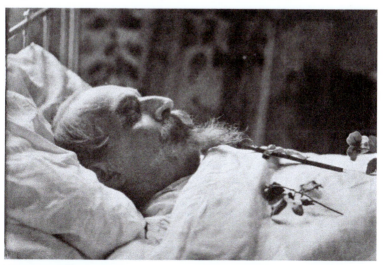

Napoleon III's death bed, 10 January 1873, in Chislehurst, Kent.

With the German victory at Sedan, most of France's existing armies were no longer participants in the war; Bazaine's Army was immobilized and besieged in the city of Metz, whilst the army led by Emperor Napoleon III himself had surrendered to the Germans. Under these circumstances the Germans hoped for an armistice which would put an official end to the hostilities and lead to peace. In particular Prussia's Minister President, Otto von Bismarck. keenly entertained that hope, as he wanted to end the war as soon as possible and concentrate on the unification of Germany. To a nation with as many neighbours as Prussia, a prolonged war meant the growing risk of intervention by another power; Bismarck was determined to limit that risk.

At first the outlook for peace seemed fair. The Germans estimated that the new Government of France would not be interested in continuing the war that had been declared by the monarch they had just deposed. Hoping to pave the road to peace, Bismarck invited the new French Government to negotiations held at Ferrières and submitted a list of moderate conditions, including limited territorial demands in Alsace.

Hostilities resume.

While the republican government was amenable to reparation payments or transfer of colonial territories in Africa or in South East Asia to Prussia, Jules Favre, on behalf of the Government of National Defence, declared on 6 September that France would not 'yield an inch of its territory nor a stone of its fortresses'. The republic then renewed the declaration of war, called for recruits in all parts of the country, and pledged to drive enemy troops out of France.

The Germans had no other option left but to continue the war under these circumstances; at the same time they could not pin down any significant military opposition in the vicinity of their concentrations of troops. As the bulk of the remaining French armies were digging-in near Paris, the German command decided to put pressure on the enemy by attacking the capital. In October, German troops reached its outskirts, which was a heavily fortified city. The Germans quickly surrounded it and established a blockade, as at Metz, by 19 September; Metz, however, surrendered on 27 October.

Losing patience, in early January 1871 the Germans overcame their qualms about bombarding a city with so many civilians in it and started shelling the city into submission, firing 12,000 shells in three weeks. They had yet to bring up heavy siege guns and killed fewer than one hundred Parisians, which had little impact on Parisian morale. However, morale plummeted when the city stood on the verge of starvation. No relief came and many Parisians, especially the working classes, unaware of the

Paris in ruins, Rue de Rivoli, 1871.

guerrilla warfare harrying German communications or the suffering of newly-raised French armies, felt deserted by France. In the end, the city capitulated on 28 January 1871. The Treaty of Versailles of 1871 ended the Franco-Prussian War and was signed by Adolphe Thiers, of the French Third Republic, and Otto von Bismarck, of the German Empire, on 26 February 1871. For anyone who wants to learn more about this fascinating part of the War of 1870 history, see David O'Mara's forthcoming 'Paris, the Sieges and the Commune' in this series.

As well as giving the City of Strasbourg and the fortification at Metz to Germany, the Treaty of Frankfurt, signed on 10 May 1871, more importantly gave her possession of Alsace and the northern portion of Lorraine (Moselle), both of which (especially Alsace) were home to a majority of ethnic Germans and were very rich in natural resources, such as iron ore and coal. France had to pay 5,000,000,000 francs in gold, in full; one billion was to be paid in 1871, before the withdrawal of any German forces. This eventually occurred on September 1873. [The figure was the equivalent (allowing for population change) that Napoleon I had imposed on Prussia in 1807.] The loss of territory would be a source of resentment in France for years to come and contributed to public support for the First World War, in which France vowed to take back control of

The Hall of Mirrors, Versailles, France. Here Wilhelm I King of Prussia became Emperor of a united Germany, the ultimate indignity for the French people.

Alsace-Lorraine. This lust for revenge created a continual state of crisis between Germany and France, which would be one of the contributing factors in the lead up to the First World War.

German unification.
While the French government deteriorated, Bismarck succeeded in achieving his long cherished ambition of German unification on 18 January 1871. With the war all but concluded, the German princes proclaimed the German Empire at Versailles, in the Hall of Mirrors in Louis XIV's grandiose château: it was the ultimate indignity for the French people. As a consequence of the declaration, Wilhelm I, King of Prussia, became Emperor of a united Germany. The declaration combined the many independent German states and it became a federal empire. Unsurprisingly, Otto von Bismarck, Minister President – ie Prime Minister – of Prussia, became Chancellor of the Empire.

The creation of a unified German Empire ended the 'balance of power' that had been created by the Congress of Vienna in 1815 at the

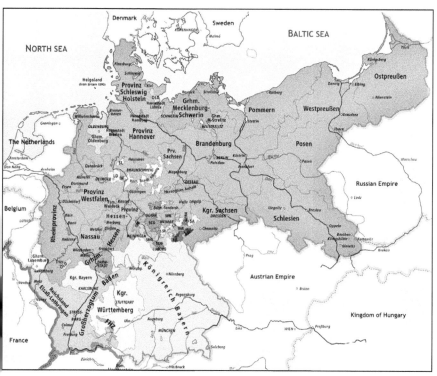

The German Empire 1871-1918. Bottom left, the annexed French department of Alsace-Lorraine.

end of the Napoleonic Wars. Countries – continental European countries in particular – previously without a General Staff or a system of universal conscription soon adopted both, along with developments in logistics, military use of railways and the telegraph system, all proven by the German victory to be indispensable and reinforcing many of the lessons learnt from the American Civil War a few years earlier. Germany quickly established itself as the leading power in Europe with the most powerful, possibly best trained and professionally best led, army in the world. Although Great Britain remained the dominant world power, by virtue of its overwhelming naval strength and its spread of colonial possessions, British involvement in European affairs during the late nineteenth century was very limited ('Splendid Isolation'), allowing Germany to exercise great influence over the European mainland. Additionally, Crown Prince Friedrich's marriage to the eldest daughter of Queen Victoria, Victoria Adelaide Mary Louise, was but one of a number of prominent German-British aristocratic marriages.

Important lessons that had been learnt for future wars were that a superior rifle, in this case the French Chassepot, in comparison with the German muzzle-loaders, could hold up an attack even when greatly outnumbered. It also proved that a modern breech loading field gun, such as the German Krupp gun, could create havoc amongst an enemy, just as the French mitrailleuses had done. These lessons would prove their 'value' in future wars and were honed to perfection in the Great War, forty or so years later.

According to the respected French historian and writer François Roth (1936-2016), he estimated the total losses of the 1870-1871 War to be: **France,** 139,000 killed or died of wounds and 143,000 wounded; **German Empire,** 45,000 killed or died of wounds and 90,000 wounded.

A much decorated but unknown French veteran of the wars of 1870-1871 and 1914-1918, photographed in 1937.

Car Tour 1

Introductory Tour:
From Buzancy to Sedan

Duration: A full day's tour
Distance: 122 kilometres
Map: IGN Aisne Ardennes D02-08, or any map that focuses on the French Ardennes.

This circular car tour covers the area south of Sedan and is designed to give a full understanding of the lay of the land for the campaign. It also features many interesting 1870 sites that otherwise would have been left out of the book because they are located too far away from the battlefields and walks. The route is accessible for all but the biggest vehicles. Because of the chronology, the tour starts in Buzancy. However, because the tour is circular, one can start at any given location and follow the route around. A pair of binoculars would be very useful as there are some spectacular views along the way. It is always advisable to take water with you. Bakeries, supermarkets and petrol stations can be found in Buzancy, Stenay, Mouzon and Sedan. Walking boots are not required.

GPS coordinates for Car Tour 1:

(1) Buzanzy, 1870 mass grave   (N49°25.632′ E004°57.561′)
(2) Buzanzy, Chanzy mortuary chapel   (N49°25.612′ E004°57.554′)
(3) Statue General Chanzy   (N49°25.581′ E004°57.336′)
(4) Buzanzy 1870 Monument   (N49°25.446′ E004°57.573′)
(5) Nouart, birthplace of General Chanzy (N49°26.346′ E005°02.876′)
(6) Nouart, statue of General Chanzy   (N49°26.440′ E005°02.964′)
(7) Mass Grave Monument   (N49°29.412′ E005°11.595′)
(8) Crimean War tomb   (N49°29.416′ E005°11.591′)
(9) Four 1870 Monuments   (N49°36.248′ E005°05.425′)
(10) French Memorial   (N49°36.262′ E005°05.408′)
(11) German Memorial   (N49°36.262′ E005°05.408′)
(12) Panorama Bazeilles-Mouzon   (N49°38.276′ E005°01.528′)
(13) Meuse Crossing at Rémilly   (N49°38.846′ E005°00.995′)

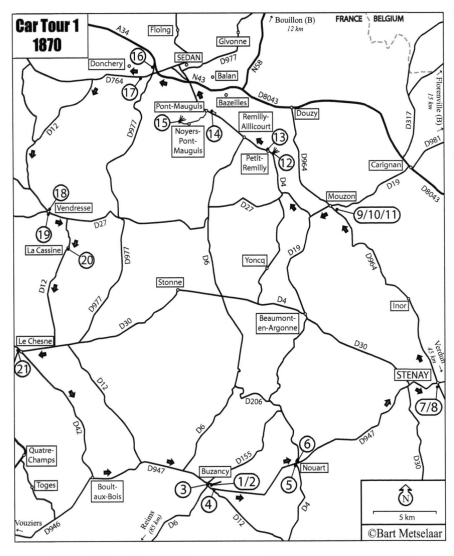

(14) Bazeilles railway bridge	(N49°39.914′ E004°58.459′)
(15) Panorama Noyers-Pont-Maugis	(N49°39.889′ E004°55.626′)
(16) Château Bellevue	(N49°41.811′ E004°54.181′)
(17) Weaver's home	(N49°41.497′ E004°52.884′)
(18) Villa La Rocques	(N49°36.329′ E004°47.710′)
(19) Château Hannonet	(N49°36.149′ E004°47.869′)
(20) Château La Cassine	(N49°34.861′ E004°48.857′)
(21) Le Chesne, HQ of Napoleon III	(N49°30.820′ E004°45.894′)

CARRE MILITAIRE

TOMBES de SOLDATS

MORTS pour la FRANCE

The mass grave in the Communal Cemetery of Buzancy.

À LA MÉMOIRE DES SOLDATS
FRANÇAIS et ALLEMANDS
Décédés en 1870
1914 - 1915

The tour starts at Buzancy Communal Cemetery (N49°25.632′ E004°57.561′), situated on the Rue du Mahomet at the outskirts of the village. Immediately after you enter the cemetery, head to the left. The **1870 Mass Grave Monument (1)** (N49°25.632′ E004°57.561′) is built in front of the wall. The French and German soldiers that are buried here were killed during the skirmish that ensued around nightfall on 27 August, when a spearhead of the French 12th Cavalry Regiment bumped into a party of Saxon cavalry. It is unknown how many soldiers were laid to rest here.

Very unusually, **General Chanzy's Mortuary Chapel (2)** (N49°25.612′ E004°57.554′) is built half in and half out of the cemetery. The reason for this is unknown. Note the First World War shell damage on the outer walls of the chapel, most notably on the right side. Also note the Oriental influences in the architecture. Chanzy did not play a role during the campaigns in Metz or Sedan, but had proved to be a more than capable general in Algeria, one of France's African colonies across the Mediterranean. On 6 December 1870, after the French defeat at Sedan,

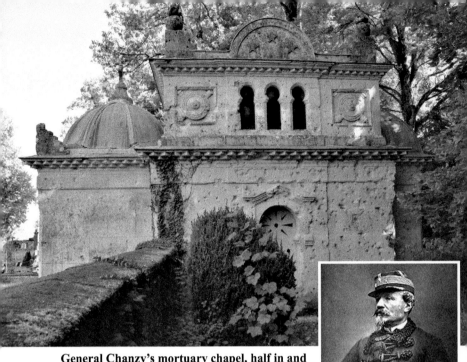

**General Chanzy's mortuary chapel, half in and
half out of the cemetery. Note the shell damage
that dates from the First World War.**

General Chanzy, 1823-1883.

Chanzy took command of XVII and XVIII Corps, forming the Second
Army of the Loire. After several battles, most notably the Battle of Le
Mans on 10-11 January 1871, the Army of the Loire was withdrawn from
action and was eventually disbanded after the signing of the Armistice
on 28th February 1871.

After the war was over, like many high-ranking military men, Chanzy
became interested in local and national politics and eventually became
General Consul of the Ardennes region. In 1873 Chanzy bought a small
château in Buzancy, not far from Nouart, his birth place. The same year,
he accepted the office of Governor of Algeria where, in spite of his new
home, he stayed for the next six years. On his return Château Chanzy
became a refuge for him and his family, a safe haven far away from the
complex political intrigue of Paris. He continued living here until his
death in 1883; during the night of 4-5 January General Chanzy died of a
cerebral hemorrhage in Châlons-en-Champagne. Château Chanzy,
currently called Château de Buzancy, lies only a few hundred yards south-
east of the cemetery. In 1982 the family property was sold to the
Department of the Ardennes, which turned the building into a lycée, a

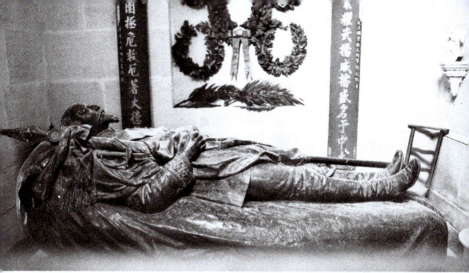

Tomb of General Chanzy.

high (secondary) school. The school closed in 2014, and at the time of writing (2019) the building is still for sale. It stands on a hill on the left side of the D947. You can just catch a glimpse of the château whilst driving to stop (3).

Return to your car and take the third road (D947) on the left, appropriately called Rue du Général Chanzy, to the town centre of Buzancy. Here, on the inevitable Place du Général Chanzy, you will find a bronze **statue of General Chanzy (3)** (N49°25.581′ E004°57.336′), Buzancy's most famous inhabitant.

Continue along the D947 for about 200 metres. Park your car on the pavement by the last house on the right hand side of the street but pay attention to the high kerb. Continue on foot for about thirty metres along the pavement until you arrive at the **Buzanzy 1870 Monument (4)** (N49°25.446′

Statue of General Chanzy in the village square in Buzancy.

E004°57.573′). The monument was erected soon after the war to commemorate the French soldiers and civilians that were killed in the skirmish of 17 August.

Face the monument and look to your right; on the other side of the street you can see an old road sign with a distinctive blue surround; note

the Second World War shell damage on the wall, the road sign and on the 1870 Monument. In June 1940 several houses along the present-day D947 were blown up by the French Army, hoping thereby to delay the spearheads of Heinz Guderian's 19th (Armoured) Division that were on their way to Rheims and Paris.

Return to the car. Continue along the D947 in the direction of Nouart/Stenay. Once within the village limits (indicated by the sign 'Nouart'), take a right turn onto the D4, the Route de Barricourt. The first house on the right is the **birth place of General Chanzy (5)** (N49°26.346′ E005°02.876′), a fact that is commemorated (facing the front door) by a tiny plaque on the right hand wall of the house. Antoine Alfred Eugène Chanzy was born on 18 March 1823 to a family of farmers. His father and uncle served under Napoleon I and were part of the Cuirassiers, French cavalry. During the Napoleonic Wars his father rose to the rank of sergeant, whilst his uncle was commissioned and ended the war as a captain. For his distinguished service, Chanzy's father was awarded the order of the Chevalier de la Legion d'Honneur, the Knight's Legion of Honour. This military award was instituted by Napoleon in 1802. Growing up around two former members of Napoleon's former Grande Armée, it was inevitable that Chanzy would follow in the footsteps of his father. After successfully completing his studies at St. Cyr Military Academy, he was commissioned in the Zouaves

1870 memorial in Buzancy. Note the shell or bullet damage from 1940.

maison natale du
GÉNÉRAL
CHANZY
1823 ~ 1883

Chanzy's birth place in Nouart.

in 1843. He participated in a good deal of fighting in Algeria, and was promoted lieutenant in 1848, and captain in 1851. He became a battalion commander in 1856 and served in the Second Italian War of Independence, amongst many other campaigns.

Initially Chanzy was not involved in the Franco-German conflict. However, after the defeat of the French Army at Sedan and the abdication of Napoleon III, revolution broke out in Paris. At the instigation of Marshal MacMahon, the government of national defence recalled him from Algeria, promoted him to general of division, and gave him command of the Army of the Loire. Interestingly, the Army of the Loire fought some of France's most successful battles of the war; but it was too little too late.

Return to your car and go across the D947 into the Rue de la Chise and continue to the church where, opposite the village war monument, there is a **statue of General Chanzy (6)** (N49°26.440′ E005°02.964′). In contrast to his bronze statue in Buzancy, a more or less contemporary monument – it was unveiled in 1886 – this one was inaugurated on 22 October 1966 in the presence of the Governor of Metz, the Prefect of the Ardennes and the Mayor and community of Nouart.

Go back to the main road, and drive along the D947 to Stenay. This takes approximately fifteen minutes. Once at the crossroads in Stenay, take a left turn and follow this road until you are at the roundabout. Here, you must take a right turn onto the D964, direction Verdun. At the second roundabout, continue straight on; after about 100 metres you will come to Stenay Communal Cemetery, on your right. Stop at the parking space at the second (centre) entrance. The **Mass Grave Monument (7)** (N49°29.412′ E005°11.595′), an obelisk, stands right in front of you. The memorial commemorates 'the 35 children of Stenay who died for France' during the battles of Beaumont and Mouzon. Today, the exact burial place and the names of the victims remain unknown but somewhere there has to be a mass grave within the walls of this cemetery. Most of the military graves dating from before 1914 have disappeared, victims of the lack of space in the churchyard.

The 1870 monument in Stenay. (T. Otte)

A little to the right of the 1870 Monument lies another interesting monument. This is the **Crimean War tomb (8)** (N49°29.416′ E005°11.591′) of Second Lieutenant Henri Misler. Born in 1828 in Stenay, he was the flag bearer of the 18th Infantry Regiment.

He was killed in Sevastopol in the Crimea on 8 September 1855 and was posthumously awarded the Imperial Knight's Cross of the Legion of Honour. It is extremely rare to find a headstone dating from the Crimean War (1853-1856) period, as the usual policy for any army was to bury the dead in mass graves where they fell. Henri must have been a member of a wealthy family, one that could afford to repatriate his body over 4,000 kilometres by boat and train to Stenay. Unfortunately no additional information could be found and no distant relatives with the name Misler appear to live in the area.

Henri Misler's headstone. (T. Otte)

114

Return to your car, make a U-turn and continue your way along the D964 in the direction of Mouzon/Sedan. Before you enter Mouzon you will see Mouzon Communal

Cemetery on the right hand side of the road. The entrance is at the southern corner, complete with a parking space in front of it. In the back of this small cemetery, built next to the large one, are **four 1870 monuments (9)** (N49°36.248′ E005°05.425′). They are

flanked by two French 1914 graves. On the first monument, **9a**, the inscription is barely legible; it, remembers eighty-eight French soldiers who died while trying to cross the River Meuse at Mouzon. They did not necessarily die from bullet wounds or shrapnel. Most soldiers simply could not swim (nor could many read or write,

German 1870 memorial.

Military plot in Mouzon Communal Cemetery.

for that matter) and drowned falling off footbridges etc. Right behind the first monument stands a second French monument, **9b**. The crucifix is dedicated to the French soldiers and civilians that died in Mouzon on 30 August 1870. As usual, the civilians suffered heavily during the war.

The two monuments behind the French monuments are German; the first one, **9c**, remembers all German soldiers that were killed during the 1870 campaign. The last of the four monuments, **9d**, is dedicated to nine different battalions and regiments. The names are almost illegible and are therefore included in full. The stone slab reads: *Magd[eburg] Inf. 27, 1Thur[inger] Inf. 31, Schlesw[ig] Holst[ein] Fus[ilier] Reg. No 86 Anh[alt], Inf. Reg. No 93 Thur[ingen], Inf. Reg. No 96 Magd[enburg], Feld Art. Reg no ??, Konigl[icher] Sachs[ische] Inf. Reg. No 100-101-105-108, Sachs[ische] Jäg[er] Bat. No 2.* Of course, it remains unknown how many soldiers of these regiments and battalions were killed or where they are buried. Most likely they are interred in mass or field graves along the German axis of advance.

Walk through the opening in the wall and enter the larger cemetery. Take the first path on your right; after about thirty metres, on the left, you will see two memorials with green, cast iron, fences. The first is a **French Memorial (10)** (N49°36.262′ E005°05.408′) dedicated to 'the memory of the soldiers who were killed in 1870', erected by the people of Mouzon. Opposite the French memorial there is a **German Memorial (11)** (N49°36.262′ E005°05.408′) that was erected to commemorate the fallen of the 27th and 31st Infantry Regiments, the 4th Artillery Regiment and the 7th Battalion of the 1st Bayrische (Bavarian) Regiment. Also mentioned is Second Lieutenant Eugen Ott, 7th Battery, Königliches Bayrische Armee [Royal Bavarian Army].

Return to your car, continue for about 100 metres and take a left turn to Mouzon centre. Drive through the medieval gate. After a hundred metres a bridge crosses the Canal de l'Est. Mouzon is built on an island in the River Meuse and dates back to pre Roman times. Follow the main road around the church. At the T-junction, take a left and continue to the second bridge. This is the approximate site of the battle that took place between

French 1870 memorial, Mouzon.   German 1870 memorial, Mouzon.

the Prussian army and General de Failly's V Corps after the French retreat from Beaumont on 30 August. Many houses in the town centre were burnt to the ground during the battle. Continue along this Roman Road, cross the railway line and after another 200 metres take a right turn onto the D27, direction Autrecourt/Rémilly/Sedan. You will see many bunkers, some very impressive, whilst driving along this scenic route to Sedan. They were built in the 1930s and form part of the Maginot Line.

After Villers-devant-Mouzon, the road changes from the D27 into the D4. Two kilometres after you have left Villers-devant-Mouzon, at the top of a hill is the 'Aire de la Cabrette'. This is the site of a magnificent **panoramic view (12)** (N49°38.276′ E005°01.528′) across the Meuse Valley. On the left side of the D4, just before the view point, lies a disused stretch of tarmac; you can easily park your car here. Cross the D4 and walk to the view-point. The site also features a sturdy wooden bench and

table, so if the weather permits this is an excellent place for a picnic. From here you can appreciate views ranging from Bazeilles on the left to Mouzon on the right. Imagine tens of thousands of soldiers and endless rows of ammunition carts, the noise they made, the dust, a mass of movement on both sides of the River Meuse in the direction of Sedan, just a few kilometres to the north-west of Bazeilles. You are on the left bank, the French side of the River; however, on the afternoon of Wednesday 31 August the advance guard of General Von der Tann's I (Bavarian) Corps, were already closing in on Sedan along the left bank of the River Meuse.

Go back to your car; after a kilometre you enter Petit Rémilly. Take the main road on the right to enter the village. Just follow the road until you are at the Bailey Bridge. This bridge was built by the French army after the Second World War. Park in front of the bridge and continue on foot to the other side of it. Look north, parallel to the Canal de L'Est. This is the area where, during the night of 31 August, Douay's VII Corps, Ducrot's I Corps and General Bonnemain's 2nd Reserve Cavalry Division **crossed the River Meuse (13)** (N49°38.846′ E005°00.995′) over flooded and half sunken pontoon bridges. Bright fires were burning on either side of the bridges to shed a little light in the pitch black night. Inevitably, several men who fell into the cold water were carried away by the strong current and were drowned.

Continue along the D4; as you pass through Rémilly-Allicourt the road number changes into the D6. Stay on the D6 until you reach

The bridge over the River Meuse at Rémilly.

The railway bridge at Bazeilles in the left distance.

Allicourt. Here, take the first road to the right, the D129, direction Bazeilles. After you have crossed the railway line there is a parking space on your left. Walk in the direction of the bridge. Just before the bridge take a left turn, but be careful, as this is a cycling path. After a short walk along the old tow path of the Canal de l'Est you come to a lock. From here, you have an excellent view of **Bazeilles railway bridge (14)** (N49°39.914′ E004°58.459′) to the left and of the town of Bazeilles itself on the right.

Here the spearheads of General von der Tann's I (Bavarian) Corps, closing in on Sedan from the left bank of the River Meuse, discovered the intact railway bridge leading to Bazeilles. On the afternoon of Wednesday 31 August, close to the bridge abutment on the far right, the fighting for Bazeilles – and consequently Sedan – started. It was here where a French demolition party, tasked with the destruction of the bridge, was surprised by Bavarian soldiers. After a brief fight the French made off and left the bridge intact for the Germans.

Return to the D6 and continue in the direction of Pont Maugis. Here, take a left turn to Noyers-Pont-Maugis, the D229, and follow the signs *Cimetière Militaire.* Take a right turn at the roundabout, onto the D229A. Once you have reached the T-junction in Noyers-Pont-Maugis you have two options; the left fork takes you to a massive German Cemetery that honours 26,843 soldiers who were killed during the two world wars.

Sedan **Balan** M

Panorama looking from La Marfée Hill over the Sedan battlefield.

However, the right fork takes you to **Marfeé Hill (15)** (N49°39.889′ E004°55.626′), from where King Wilhelm of Prussia and his retinue were watching events unfold before their eyes. On 1 September 1870, with the aid of powerful binoculars, the Prussian high command and journalists from all over Europe watched the outcome of the battle for Sedan in detail. The original spot is on the north-western side of Marfeé Hill but this is not easy accessible to the public. Conveniently for the visitor today, an observation platform has been built close to the parking space. There are several information panels that provide information about the three wars that were fought in this area over a period of seventy-five years. Adjacent to the parking space is the French La Marfeé War Cemetery, which holds the remains of 1,723 soldiers from two world wars, including twelve Commonwealth War Graves. Unopposed, the Germans crossed the River Meuse in Sedan again on 27 August 1914 and on 12 May 1940. One can only wonder.

Return to the main road (D6) in Noyers-Pont-Maugis and turn left in the direction of Wadelincourt/Sedan. Just after you have passed the flyover, take the left fork of the T-junction until you are at the junction of the D6/D8043A. Turn left to Frénois/Donchéry. At the second roundabout take a right turn onto the D29; after about 500 metres you are at **Château Bellevue (16)** (N49°41.811′ E004°54.181′). The safest place to park is on the grass opposite the Château. *Please note that the château is private property.*

In this château, on 2 September 1870, in the presence of Bismarck, von Moltke and King Wilhelm of Prussia, Napoleon III and General de Wimpffen signed the official military capitulation of Sedan and the Army of Châlons. It is important to appreciate that Napoleon did NOT sign the

Bazeilles   Mouzon ⟶

Château Bellvue, where Napoleon surrendered Sedan and the Army of Châlons.

capitulation of France. It had been argued that this at least partly explains why the war dragged on for another four months; however, given the ferment in Paris at the time and the abandonment of the empire for a new republic almost as soon as the news of the armistice signed in Sedan reached the capital, the view is doubtful.

Drive back to the roundabout and take the D764, direction Donchéry. After approximately one kilometre, the **Weaver's Home (17)** (N49°41.497′ E004°52.884′) is situated on the left of the road, just as you arrive at the first houses of the village. The site is signposted on the

The weaver's home, then and now. The caption on the 'then' postcard states that Napoleon and Bismarck met on the first floor, in the room that has the open window; other accounts suggest that they met just outside the house.

right side of the road, but is very easy to miss. You can park next to the signpost. *Please note that the house is private property.*

After the capitulation of Sedan on 1 September 1870, negotiations started at von Moltke's HQ in the mayor's house in Donchéry about the terms of surrender. The negotiations ended unsatisfactorily. In the early morning of 2 September, Napoleon decided to take matters into his own hands. He set off to Donchery, where both parties agreed to use this simple weaver's home as a meeting place. Again it proved impossible to come to an agreement and the negotiations were once more postponed. Today, it is hard to imagine that Bismarck, Moltke and Napoleon sat on wooden chairs in front of this house, making decisions that would determine the fate of Europe for much of the next century.

Continue along the D764 until you reach the hamlet of Pont-à-Bar, which also has a small marina. Here, take a left, the D12, to Sapogne/Vendresse. When you reach Vendresse, take the first street on the left, the Rue de la Halle, where, on the right and at the far end of the street, you will see the **Villa La Rocques (18)** (N49°36.329′ E004°47.710′). From 31 August to 4 September 1870, this now rather sad looking château, which could do with 'elements of refurbishment', was the HQ of Bismarck.

Villa La Roques, Bismarck's HQ for several days.

Return to the main road and turn left. Just before the third road on the right, at Rue Pol Bouin 60, you will come to the gate of **Château Hannonet (19)** (N49°36.149′ E004°47.869′). King Wilhelm of Prussia and von Moltke's HQ was located in the buildings you see when looking through the gate. King Wilhelm enjoyed the comforts of Vendresse from 31 August to 4 September 1870. From Vendresse the commander in chief of the German army travelled up and down to the front line.

Château Hannonet, King Wilhelm's HQ.

Two kilometres further along the D12 lie the ruins of **Château La Cassine (20)** (N49°34.861′ E004°48.857′). This Empire-style château dates from 1850 and was built on top of the ruins of Château de Louis de Gonzague (1572). From 31 August to 4 September 1870 the building was in use by Crown Prince Frederick of Prussia and his staff. As a snippet of information and for what it is worth, from a letter that Bismarck wrote to D. Moritz Busch, dated 31 August, we know that he joined the king, the crown prince and Moltke for dinner here; he had scrambled eggs and a sandwich, so it was hardly a feast.

In 1927 a small part of the château was destroyed by fire after a dispute between a servant and the Camion family but it remained largely intact. The family was not that lucky in 1939. After the mobilization of France on 2 September 1939, a garrison of French soldiers occupied part of the château to guard the crossings of the Canal des Ardennes that was dug behind the building in 1830. While preparing a meal, disaster struck when the soldiers

Château La Cassine, Frederick of Prussia's HQ.

accidentally set fire to a room that ultimately led to the almost total destruction of Château La Cassine, although some impressive ruins remain.

Continue for ten kilometres along the D12 in the direction of Le Chesne. At the T-junction turn right onto the D977 until you are in the centre of the village. On 28 August 1870, Napoleon III spent a night in the inn that is now called La Charrue d'Or, the Golden Plough **(21)** (N49°30.820′ E004°45.894′). You can park in front of the bar. Today, the facade is barely recognisable when compared to that of 1870 as the whole premises have been redeveloped. If you cross the bridge you can compare the then and now photographs in the book. Turn your car and continue on the D42, direction Châtillon. Stay on this road until you come to the junction of the D42/D947, where you take a left to return to Buzancy, the starting point of this circular tour.

Le Chesne, then and now: Napoleon III stayed in the building marked with a cross above it on the postcard and behind the car on the modern photograph.

Walk 1

Beaumont

Duration: half a day's tour
Distance: eleven kilometres
Map: IGN 3110 O Carignan.

The tour starts and ends at Beaumont Communal Cemetery. You can park your car in the parking space opposite the entrance to the cemetery (N49°32.412′ E005°03.438′). Be sure not to block the gates of the local residents. At the time of writing, there is a tiny 'Proxi' supermarket behind the Mairie, open daily from 7.45 am to 12.15 pm, and on weekdays only from 16.30 pm to 19.30 pm. There are no public restrooms along the way. NOTE: For this walk you have to be in a good physical condition. About 70% of the walk follows tarmac roads or well-maintained tracks, but between stop (10) and (13) there is no path or track; this part of the tour follows the edge of a forest and sometimes you have to be a bit resourceful to find your way. Do not enter fields with livestock. Sturdy walking boots are recommended and it is also useful to take water and a pair of binoculars with you. Beware of ticks – trousers and reasonably thick socks are recommended.

GPS coordinates Walk 1:

(1) Ignace Brinder Monument	(N49°32.414′ E005°03.330′)
(2) Max Wilke Monument	(N49°32.416′ E005°03.333′)
(3) French V Corps Monument	(N49°32.417′ E005°03.336′)
(4) Charles Mathis Fr. Monument	(N49°32.420′ E005°03.328′)
(5) German Monument	(N49°32.425′ E005°03.360′)
(6) Wilhelm Hasse Monument	(N49°32.425′ E005°03.360′)
(7) Church	(N49°32.301′ E005°03.438′)
(8) River crossing	(N49°32.221′ E005°03.488′)
(9) Panorama	(N49°31.501′ E005°03.937′)
(10) German Chapel	(N49°31.135′ E005°04.001′)
(11) Panorama	(N49°31.086′ E005°03.555′)
(12) Panorama	(N49°31.197′ E005°03.157′)

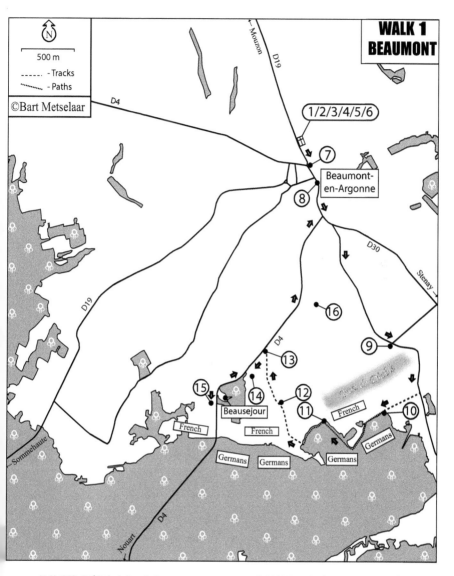

(13) US 2nd Division Monument	(N49°31.430′ E005°03.905′)
(14) Mass Grave	(N49°31.313′ E005°03.009′)
(15) IR 96 Monument	(N49°31.160′ E005°02.670′)
(16) IR 86 Monument	(N49°31.616′ E005°03.387′)

The tour starts at Beaumont Communal Cemetery (N49°32.412′ E005°03.438′). The cemetery has six monuments relating to the Franco-Prussian War. Enter the cemetery. Monuments 1-4 can be easily found as they are situated along first the path on the left.

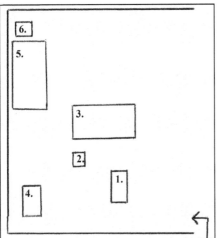

The Communal Cemetery in Beaumont.

Plan of the 1870 monuments in Beaumont cemetery.

The first of the six 1870 monuments in this cemetery is that of **Ignace Brinder (1)** (N49°32.414′ E005°03.330′). It is easily recognizable by the green wrought iron fence that is so characteristic of French 1870 graves. Brinder was a soldier of the 3rd Company, 86th Regiment, which was part of General Failly's V Corps. During the fighting around Beaumont on 30 August 1870 Brinder was seriously wounded. According to the inscription on his headstone, he 'died gloriously of his wounds on 22 October'. We can assume

Grave of Ignace Brinder.

Grave of Max Wilke with inscription detail.

that Brinder, like countless other soldiers, suffered terribly for weeks on end before he finally 'gloriously' succumbed to his injuries.

A little to the left of Brinders' monument, there is the Latin cross headstone of **Max Wilke (2)** (N49°32.416′ E005°03.333′). Hauptman Wilke, born on 2 October 1836, was part of the 26th Regiment of the I Magdeburger Division. Mortally wounded on 30 August, he died of wounds on 3 September 1870.

Behind Wilke's headstone stands the **French V Corps Monument (3)** (N49°32.417′ E005°03.336′). This is the central French monument that commemorates all the French soldiers that were involved in the Battle of Beaumont. Divisions and regiments that were involved in the carnage are remembered on the side panels. On its rear four soldiers are particularly remembered; they were born in Beaumont and were killed during the battle.

The French V Corps Monument.

Grave of Charles Mathis with inscription detail.

At the far left corner of the cemetery (see the cemetery plan at Stop 1) you will find the metal monument of **Charles Mathis (4)** (N49°32.420′ E005°03.328′). Mathis was a battalion commander in the 86th Infantry Regiment and was mortally wounded on 30 August. He died three days later in a field hospital in Beaumont. At the opposite corner of the cemetery, to the left and at the back, stands a magnificent **German Monument (5)** (N49°32.425′ E005°03.360′) that is dedicated to the officers of the 26th and 66th Magdeburger Regiments who were killed on 30 August. The names of the officers are listed on stone panels on both sides of the central text. Interestingly, the panels also mention on the one 197 and on the other 104 non-commissioned and soldiers who were buried at Culée Mozet. Unfortunately, and in spite of extensive research, this location could not be found. The bronze plaque that has been placed in front of the monument reveals some interesting details. According to this, the officers mentioned on the stone slab on the left were buried in this cemetery. Any record of their location has been lost over time, but it is assumed that they lie buried at this spot. The plaque also records thirteen non-commissioned officers and 167 soldiers who were buried on the battlefield, *Es ruhen auf dem Schlachtfelde*; their location is now unknown.

Magdeburger Memorial with inscription details.

DEM·GEDAECHTNISSE
DER·AM·30.AUGUST·1870
GEFALLENEN·OFFIZIERE
DER·MAGDEBURGISCHEN
INFANTERIE·REGIMENTER
№·2 Gu.66.

DEN·HELDENTOD·STARBEN
VOM·MAGDEB.INF·REGT. №GG
Oberstleutnant
GRAF FINCK VON FINCKENSTEIN
VON BREDOW   HAUPTMANN
BONSAC   „
VON DOSSOW   „
SCHROEDER   PREM-LEUTNANT
STEINBART   „   „
VON TROTT   „   „
VON HERTELL   „   „
KAEMPFE   SEKON-LEUTNANT
VON BOCKUM DOLFFS „ „
VON STEINAECKER   „ „
197 UNTEROFFIZ. U. MANNSCHAFTEN
RUHEN BEI CULÉE MOZET.

Next to the German monument lies the grave marker of Lieutenant Colonel **Wilhelm Hasse (6)** (N49°32.425′ E005°03.360′). He was born on 21 November 1820 and was killed, aged 49 years, on the

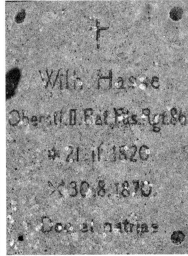

Grave of Lieutenant Colonel Wilhelm Hasse with detail of inscription.

battlefield of Beaumont on 30 August 1870. He was related to the Wehrmacht General Wilhelm Hasse (1894-1945). Note the beautiful quality of the cast iron cross and wreath.

Leave the cemetery and turn left along the D19 in the direction of the **Church (7)** (N49°32.301′ E005°03.438′). The first stone for this impressive building was laid in the twelfth century. On 30 August 1870 and during the days thereafter, overseen by the parish priest, Abbé Defourny, the church served as a hospital. The heavily wounded were put on the ground in the left and right aisles; these were mostly men that could not be saved. They suffered from severed limbs, broken bones, bullet holes and/or sword cuts, among other things. Nine out of ten wounded simply bled to death on the church floor. The nave was transformed into a space that at least had the appearance of a hospital; the church benches were all taken outside and replaced by straw mattresses. Nurses ran around with hot water and bandages, some engaged in making the latter by cutting into strips bed linen requisitioned from the village. The few doctors did everything in their power to help the wounded but there were simply too many casualties. Hundreds of soldiers perished on the battlefield. No one had expected a battle of this magnitude in Beaumont. The bodies were buried in large mass graves as

The church of Beaumont.

soon as possible after death was confirmed; but not, it seems, before every one of them had been ransacked and robbed of their last, pitiful, earthly possessions.

Should the church doors be open, a visit inside is well worthwhile. On the right wall, close to the south transept, are several war-related memorials. Another interesting fact is that in the seventeenth century Louis XIV (1638-1715), better known as the Sun King, donated money to replace the altar in the church. *NOTE: should the door be locked, you can ask for the key at Number 15, Rue du Mairie, one of the row of houses across the street, opposite the entrance of the church.*

The plaque inside the church that remembers the fallen.

Leave the church and continue along the D30, direction Stenay. As you have left the last buildings behind, you reach the metal railing of a **bridge (8)** (N49°32.221′ E005°03.488′) that crosses a nameless creek, a tributary of the River Meuse. On 30 August 1870, eye witness Felix Dahn recorded: *Just outside the little town, on the left side of the road near a large stone bridge, there were 900 French prisoners. Among them was a*

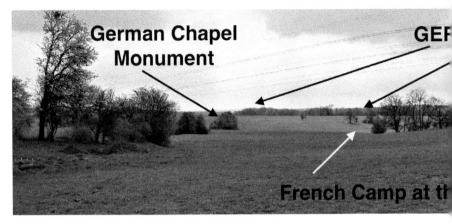

German Chapel Monument **GER** **French Camp at th**

priest who had been caught firing at the Germans; he was to be executed in the next hour or so. The prisoners were in a field to your immediate left, just across the bridge. It is easy to understand why the Germans used this spot for their prisoners; the field is partially bounded by a ridge and a creek.

The bridge in Beaumont.

Continue along the D30 for a few hundred metres and take the second road to the right. This road takes you past a farm house and barns, and is a main road. The guard dogs at the farm are (whenever I have visited) chained to a barn. After about two kilometres, close to the high voltage pylon and a seemingly permanent huge pile of manure, you come to the highest point of the ridge. From here you have a great view across the battlefield. Use the **Panoramic view (9)** (N49°31.501′ E005°03.937′) for orientation. It is quite clear from this elevated position to appreciate that the French were in a very disadvantageous situation. The French bivouacked in the 'Trou du Diable', the Devil's Hole, a valley that runs parallel with the forest. If you look back from where you are standing now, you can see Beaumont in the distance. Compare the views with the photograph in the book.

POSITIONS

om of the Ravine

View back towards Beaumont.

Walk on for 1,500 metres until you see a track on your right. This track leads to the **German Chapel (10)** (N49°31.135′ E005°04.001′). The chapel remembers the fallen of the Magdeburger 26th and 66th Regiments, who are probably buried in a mass grave close to this memorial. In 2011 the monument was restored by the German Reservisten-Marsch-& Arbeitsgruppe from Nordrhein-Westfalen/Hessen and is looked after by the German War Graves Commission. This is the only non-national 1870 monument that has been restored by the Germans

DEM GEDRECHTNISS·
DER·1870·GEFALLENEN·
DEUTSCHEN·SOLDATEN·
DER·MAGD·INF·REG·N⁰·26·66·
+·MAGD·FELD·ART·REG·N⁰·4·

The German Memorial Chapel with detail of the inscription.

that I know of; all the other German monuments have been cared for by the French *Souvenir Français*, an organization that since 1906 has taken care of military monuments and graves from all wars. To the immediate left of the chapel are the remains of trenches dating from the First World War.

Now the difficult part of the walk starts. Carry on along the trail next to the chapel for another hundred metres until you are past the clearing (pylon). The best approach is to carry on along the edge of the forest; a low embankment surrounding the entire forest shows you the way. When you enter the forest, keep this bank on your right hand at all times. Sometimes your path will be blocked by a fallen tree, shrubberies or thick undergrowth; go around the obstruction and return to the bank. After a kilometre or so of forestry terrain you will arrive at the corner of the woods. From this position, there is a great view across the valley, the Devil's Hole, see **Panorama (11)** (N49°31.086' E005°03.555'). At the time French tents were pitched everywhere and uniforms taken off to dry out. Fires to make coffee were started down at the creek that flows on the bottom of the valley floor. The whole area was crammed with men, horses, ammunition carts and the like. All of a sudden the whole valley

Le Trou du Diable, the Devil's Hole.

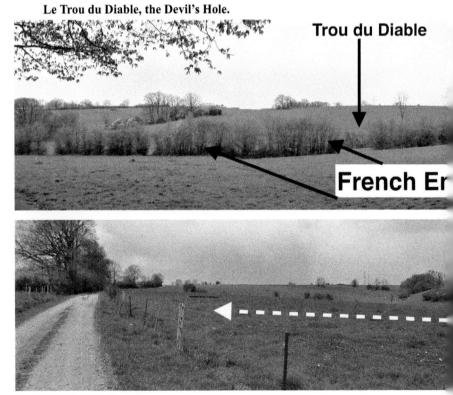

The French Camp.

was in flames; shells were exploding and the crackling of rifle fire seemed to come from all directions. In several places the Germans tried to rush the French camp from the edge of the forest, but the French soldiers reacted surprisingly quickly and put up a stiff fight. The rapid-firing Chassepot rifle caused many casualties and the Germans broke of the assault. If you look at the valley, you wonder how anyone could escape from this death trap.

Continue along the bank until you come to a small stream. Cross the stream (there is no bridge) and turn right. The French camp was on both sides of the track. After about 200 metres you will obtain a clear view of the valley, see **Panorama (12)** (N49°31.197′ E005°03.157′).

At the end of the track, when you reach the tarmac of the D4, you come to the **US 2nd Division Monument (13)** (N49°31.430′ E005°03.905′). Erected soon after the Armistice, many of these monuments were placed along the lines of advance of the 2nd Division. Originally there used to be a copper information panel bolted to the monuments, but they have long gone. This boulder commemorates the furthest point of advance on 2 November 1918.

After the Americans broke through the Hindenburg Line (the German main line of resistance in the Meuse during the First World War) on 14

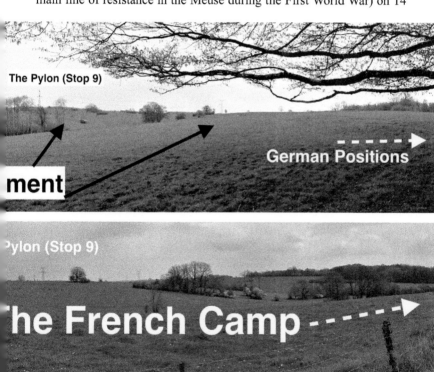

October 1918 around Romagne, the German defences gradually crumbled. From early November German troops in this area retreated to the River Meuse to develop a new line of defence. On 2 November the German 88th Division was undertaking a fighting retreat to Beaumont. It took up positions in Belval Wood; but this time, forty-eight years after the events of 1870, it was American artillery that shelled the Germans occupying the woods and valleys around Beaumont. In spite of initial American success, the fighting was difficult and costly, mainly because of deadly and accurate German shell fire. The Germans eventually evacuated Beaumont during the night of 5-6 November 1918.

The American 2nd Division Monument, 1920.

Turn left onto the D4 and walk along the tarmac road. In the field on your left, behind the copse where the 2nd Division Monument stands, you can see a **mass grave monument (14)** (N49°31.313′ E005°03.009′). *NOTE: Do NOT enter when there are cows in the field.*

The inscription, in French, reads: *To Captain Albert Roth, Captain Xavier de Hilger, Lieutenant Ruppert and many Bavarian soldiers, 30-8-1870.* This is possibly the only monument in the Sedan area that has been erected by the French to commemorate the Germans. It clearly indicates that there is a mass grave in this field, which is extremely rare, as these locations have usually been lost over time.

German mass grave.

About 500 metres further along the D4 you will come to an abandoned farm on your left. This is the site of Tuillerie Farm. A little further on, a farm track starts on the right side of the road. After about thirty metres, on the right side of the track, you will come to the **7 IR 96 Monument (15)** (N49°31.160′ E005°02.670′).

Thüringer Monument.

138

Sometimes it can be hard to find, especially in the summer, when it is quite possible that the monument will be completely covered by almost impenetrable blackberry bushes. This monument was erected to commemorate the members of the 7th Regiment, raised in the German province of Thüringen. This regiment was part of the 96th Division. The regiment was established in October 1807 and was involved in numerous campaigns. It was finally dissolved and disbanded after the First World War ended.

Return to the D4, turn left and walk back to Beaumont. After about a kilometre you will come to the German **IR 86 Monument (16)** (N49°31.616′ E005°03.387′) in a field on the right. *NOTE: do NOT go into the field if there are cows around.* This memorial was built to remember 'those that died a hero's death' who were members of the 86th Fusilier Regiment, from Schleswig-Holstein. From this regiment, 146 men were killed: six officers, eleven non-commissioned officers and 129 soldiers. In one day, the Germans and French suffered about 10,000 casualties, of whom 7,000 were killed.

Continue along the D4 to Beaumont; you will get back to your car in about twenty minutes.

Then and now, 1870 and 2020, with detail of the memorial's plaque.

Walk 2

Bazeilles

Duration: half a day's tour
Distance: four kilometres
Map: IGN 3010 E Raucourt-et-Flaba

This walk starts and ends at Musée de la Dernière Cartouche [Museum of the Last Cartridge], situated on the D764 (N49°40.901' E004°58.533'). The museum can easily be reached via the N43/E44 motorway from Charleville-Mézières to Sedan: Exit 3, Bazeilles, is clearly signposted. There are several shops and cafés in the centre of Bazeilles; however, shops are, as a general rule, closed between 12.00 pm and 2.00 pm. Sedan city centre is only a ten minute drive from the museum. A flash light/torch will be very useful at Stop 3.

Opening hours Musée de la Dernière Cartouche:

Open daily except Mondays and Tuesdays.
15 June-30 September: 1.30 pm to 6 pm
30 September-15 June: 1.30 pm to 5 pm
Email: museemdc@orange.fr

GPS coordinates Walk 2:

(1)	Musée de la Dernière Cartouche	(N49°40.901' E004°58.533')
(2)	French Marine Monument	(N49°40.931' E004°58.479')
(3)	Ossuary 1870	(N49°40.751' E004°58.549')
(4)	German Bavarian Monument	(N49°40.722' E004°58.413')
(5)	Ferme Turenne	(N49°40.594' E004°58.408')
(6)	Church	(N49°40.543' E004°58.582')
(7)	Mairie	(N49°40.584' E004°58.611')
(8)	Street view	(N49°40.556' E004°58.616')
(9)	Plaque Lieutenant Fougainville	(N49°40.577' E004°58.624')
(10)	Site of temporary church 1870-1913	(N49°40.519' E004°58.646')
(11)	Bazeilles Monument 1870	(N49°40.528' E004°58.667')
(12)	Château d'Orival	(N49°40.378' E004°58.860')
(13)	Café Aux Ruines de Bazeilles	(N49°40.686' E004°58.670')
(14)	Villa Beurmann	(N49°40.841' E004°58.598')

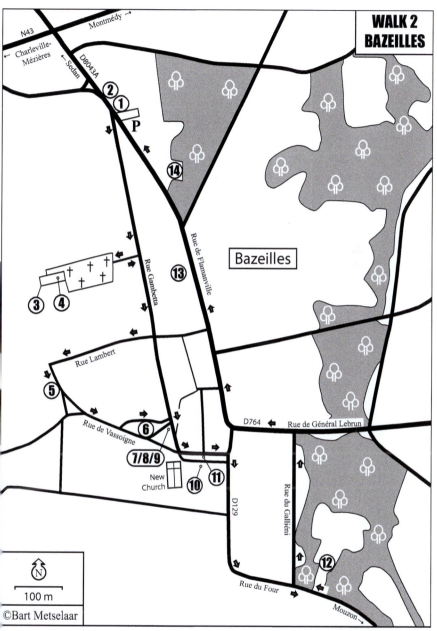

Montmédy ⟶

N43

← Charleville-Mézières

Sedan

D8043A

② ①

P

⑭

Rue Gambetta

Rue de Flamanville

Bazeilles

③ ④

⑬

Rue Lambert

⑤

Rue de Vassoigne

⑥

D764 ← Rue de Général Lebrun

7/8/9

New Church

⑩ ⑪

D129

Rue du Galliéni

⑫

Rue du Four

Mouzon ⟶

N

100 m

©Bart Metselaar

Park your vehicle in the parking space in front of the **Musée de la Dernière Cartouche (1)** (N49°40.901′ E004°58.533′). It is not a very large museum, but it is possibly amongst the most spectacular in northern France. The

BAZEILLES [ARDENNES]
31 AOUT — 1ᵉ SEPTEMBRE 1870

MAISON DE LA DERNIERE CARTOUCHE

MUSÉE

The 1870 *Musée de la Dernière Cartouche*, then and now.

collection is housed in the former Taverne Bourgerie, where on 1 September fifty French officers made a last stand against overwhelming numbers of Bavarian soldiers (see Chapter 5). Presumably, Captain Georges Aubert fired the last round (cartouche/cartridge) from a window on the first floor. When after four hours of dogged fighting the much reduced garrison of the Auberge surrendered, the way to Balan, a suburb of Sedan, was free and the taverne itself in ruins.

Not long after the battle the owners of the café/hostel started collecting material from the battlefield. The Auberge became a favorite meeting place for French 1870 veterans; in their turn they donated uniforms, helmets and weaponry to the owners. Most notable amongst these is the uniform of General Gallieni, housed in a glass case on the first floor; as a young officer he served in the 3rd Marine Infantry and fought here. He was captured and set about learning languages whilst a prisoner of war. In 1914, in the early stages of the Great War, he was the Military Governor of Paris and played a dramatic part in the defeat of the Germans on the Marne in September of that year. He went on to become Minister of War, but fell out with Joffre over Verdun, resigned and died soon afterwards.

What makes the museum, established in 1969, so special is that much of the war damage has been preserved in the building. While admiring the collection, you can still see numerous bullet holes in the ceilings, window frames, doors and walls. And if that is not enough, there is still some original bullet riddled furniture on the first floor. Also on the first floor is a large painting depicting Captain Georges Aubert firing the symbolic last bullet from a window. When you continue into the room opposite the painting you suddenly find yourself in that very room. The bed, the door, the clock; everything here breathes history and bears witness to the events in 1870. It is like going back in time and this is what makes it stand out for me from any other war museum. Strongly recommended. The curator of the museum speaks English. If, for some reason, the Ossuary, see Stop 3, is closed, you can pick up a key at the museum during opening hours. Of course, please make sure to return the key.

An impression of the interior of the museum. Note the bullet holes.

The French Marine Monument.

When you exit the museum, walk towards the D764 and turn right. Continue for about fifty metres until you come to the **French Marine Monument (2)** (N49°40.931′ E004°58.479′). The monument marks a small mass grave in which nineteen marines are buried. The monument was erected in 1873.

Walk back to the museum, cross the road, the D764, and continue to the **Ossuary 1870 (3)** (N49°40.751′ E004°58.549′) which is clearly signposted. Follow Rue Gambetta for about 300 metres. For decades this

Rue Gambetta/ Rue de la Crypte, then and now.

OSSUAIRE 1870

street was called Rue de la Crypte, Street of the Crypt. When you see the sign 'Ossuaire 1870' pointing to the right, take a look at the then and now photograph of the Rue de la Crypte.

Once at the sign, cross the street and go through the gate of the communal cemetery. The ossuary is clearly visible at the back. Officially, the ossuary is closed from October to March. However, during opening hours the key can be picked up at the museum.

The Ossuary in the early 1900s and today. Note that the German Cenotaph behind the entrance gates has been moved to the left.

Almost any visitor of the Great War battlefield of Verdun will have gone to see the Ossuary in Douaumont. There, in twenty partly underground vaults, the bones of an estimated 130,000 soldiers have been collected. Portholes at the back of the monument make it possible to take a look at the bones, an image that you will not soon forget. The Bazeilles Ossuary is rather different; it is another Douaumont Ossuary but in even more doubtful taste and something the like of which you will probably have never seen before.

You descend into the partially underground crypt, and enter a central hallway. On the left, the German side, you will find several crypts containing grave monuments and memorials. These were erected and built during the German occupation of 1914-1918. When the Germans occupied this part of France in 1914 they were absolutely horrified to discover what the French had done with the remains of these soldiers of 1870. The bodies were not buried but lay stacked, haphazardly, inside the vaults. With their well-known Teutonic thoroughness, the Germans buried their soldiers in the crypt and sealed off the graves with concrete. Fortunately they left the French cellars untouched.

On the right, the French side, the situation is presumably largely as when the human remains were originally placed here. When you look into the crypts from behind the glass, on the left and right of a narrow 'path' you see heaps of body parts mixed together. Because of the climatic conditions here, some body parts are partly mummified. Many of the remains still have fragments of skin attached to them; sometimes a whole arm, including the fingers, are clearly visible. Bones protrude from soldiers' boots, there are carcasses still with shreds of uniform on them; if you look carefully – much helped by the use of a torch – you can see the horrors of war in a quite extraordinary way, although the effect had been toned down over the passage of time, the remains collecting dust for the past 150 years.

On leaving the crypt of the ossuary you will find the **German Bavarian Monument. (4)** (N49°40.722′ E004°58.413′) on the right. This monument commemorates and marks the mass grave of 500 Bavarian soldiers that died during the fighting in Bazeilles.

The Bavarian Monument.

146

Walk back to the entrance of the cemetery and turn right. Continue along the Rue Gambetta for about 200 metres. When you arrive at the crossroads take a right turn into Ruelle du Mayot which confusingly is also named the Rue Lambert. Continue for about 200 metres and take a left at the T-junction. On the right side of the road you will see **Ferme de Turenne (5)** (N49°40.594' E004°58.408'). This fortified farm, or *château fort*, was built around 1600 at the instigation of the Prince of Sedan, Henri de la Tour d'Auvergne, Duke of Bouillon and Viscount of Turenne. The appearance of the farm has changed somewhat over the centuries but the gate, the walled courtyard on the left and the main building all date from that period.

Ferme Turenne, then and now.

During the fighting in 1870 the many embrasures were used by the French to keep the German attackers at bay but proved to be no match for the breech-loading Krupp guns. When the Germans crossed the railway bridge in ever increasing numbers the French outpost positions in Ferme de Turenne became untenable and a withdrawal to the city centre was unavoidable. The buildings were severely damaged during the fighting but restored after the war. The farm has been a scheduled monument since 1950.

Leave Turenne Farm; at the fork in the road turn left onto Rue d'en Bas, which leads back into the village. The street name later changes into Rue de Vaissoigne. After about 300 metres you will come to the Place de la Republique, a village green on the site where once the **church (6)** (N49°40.543′ E004°58.582′) stood. During the fighting the church was severely damaged by the German guns. When the fighting was over, the Germans set fire to it and to all of the surrounding buildings that had not yet been destroyed. When the Germans finally left the area, Bazeilles was entirely razed to the ground.

An eyewitness who visited the town three weeks after Napoleon's defeat at Sedan noted:

'Bazeilles was something more than a prosperous village; it must have been a flourishing town emerging into importance, with substantial stone houses, numerous wide streets, hotels, churches and large public buildings. Now, only enough remains to show what they once were. Not a house is left standing; we might almost say, metaphorically, not one stone on another. All around is a mass of desolate ruins. The meanest and the finest buildings are alike destroyed, to an extent but ill represented by the word gutted. [...]

The burnt-out shell of Bazeilles Church.

2. 1870 — BAZEILLES — La Place et l'Église au lendemain de la Bataille
S.-P., édit., L. Dufour à Reims (Marne), reproduction interdite

As now well known, the Bavarian troops returned after the battle and razed the town by firing masses of straw in each separate house. How effectually they did their work may be gathered from the fact that when we saw it, three weeks later, the ruins were still smoking. […] One old man, who had been present during the contest, described in a hoarse, choking voice the destruction of Bazeilles and the vengeance executed on the inhabitants.'

One of the civilians who had managed to escape the slaughter told an English officer:

'I'm now a pauper but I was once the principal hotel keeper in the town. As I watched the battle, I saw my house first battered and then in flames, while the Bavarians pillaged its contents, threw the provisions into the streets and set the wine running from my casks in torrents in the gutters. […] My own life was only spared because I had given drink to some wounded officers.'

Cross the field (watch out for dog dirt!) diagonally to the left. When you have reached the opposite end of the green, look across the street to the restored **Mairie. (7)** (N49°40.584′ E004°58.611′). Compare the view with the then and now photographs in the book.

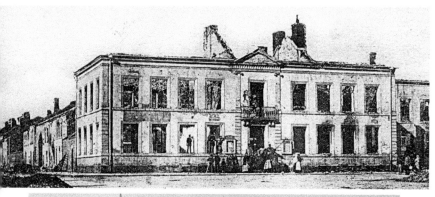

The Town Hall, then and now.

S.-P., édit., L. Dufour à Reims (Marne), reproduction interdite

The ruins of the Place de la Commune after the battle.

Standing on the same spot, look towards the supermarket and the café on the right. Compare today's view with the after the battle **street view (8)** (N49°40.556′ E004°58.616′).

Cross the street in the direction of the tiny supermarket, turn left and walk to house number 5, where you will find the commemorative **Plaque Fougainville (9)** (N49°40.577′ E004°58.624′) fixed above the door. Lieutenant Jacques Charles, Vicomte (Viscount) de Fougainville, 1st Marine Infantry Regiment, was killed on this spot. He was born in 1843, entered service in the marines in 1861, was

The house where Lieutenant Charles was killed, with the plaque above the door to the left of the car (see close up of commemorative plaque).

commissioned in 1865, was a lieutenant at the end of 1868 and was serving in Toulon with the 4th Marine Infantry Regiment in January 1869.

Retrace your steps and walk towards the new church. Turn left into the Place d'Infanterie de Marine, cross the street and walk into the parking area. You are now at the site of the **temporary church. (10)** (N49°40.519′ E004°58.646′) This house was built soon after the war was over and served as a temporary church. A wooden bell tower was erected in front of the building, see the then and now photographs. The new church, still the town parish church, was consecrated in 1912.

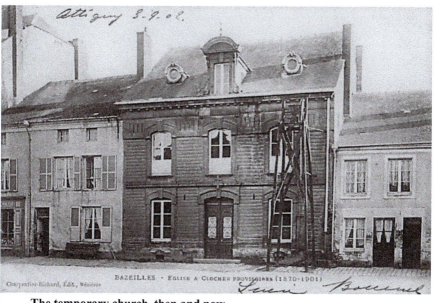

The temporary church. then and now.

The Marine Monument.

Now walk towards the **Bazeilles 1870 Monument (11)** (N49°40.528′ E004°58.667′), which is modestly located in the centre of the parking area. Besides the ossuary, this is Bazeilles'

main war memorial. It is dedicated to the men of the Marine Infantry Regiments, XII Army Corps (General Lebrun), twenty-seven adult civilians and an unknown number of children who were killed between 31 August and 1 September.

Cross the street and when you arrive at Rue du Four, the D129, turn right. Follow this road that gently curves to the left for about 400 metres until you are at the gate of **Château d'Orival (12)** (N49°40.378′ E004°58.860′), which is situated on the left side of the road.

The château was constructed in 1750 by the extremely wealthy textile baron Louis Labauche (1698-1780). Miraculously, during the fighting in Bazeilles the château was largely spared and served as a hospital for wounded Bavarian soldiers. An interesting fact is that in 1815 the future King Wilhelm I (son of the Prussian King Friedrich Wilhelm III [1770-1840, reigned 1797-1840] of Prussia) spent a few nights in the château not long after the Battle of Waterloo (18 June 1815). In 1989 the right wing of the château burnt down; today the remaining walls are 'protected' by a hideous metal construction with a corrugated iron roof.

Château Dorival, then and now.

Walk back about fifty metres, turn right into Rue Galliéni and continue along this road for about 300 metres. At the T-junction, Rue du Général Lebrun, cross the street and turn left. Follow the bend in the road to the right; this is Rue Flamanville, the D764. After about 400 metres, across the street, there is the **Café Aux Ruines de Bazeilles (13)** (N49°40.686′ E004°58.670′). As for many wars, 'battlefield' tourism started immediately after the guns fell silent. At first locals from the

Café Aux Ruines de Bazeilles.

surrounding villages came to see what had happened to Bazeilles, soon to be followed by people from all over France. Foreign journalists were also keen to report about the disaster that had hit the town. It was one of the very rare times that the destruction of a village got such intensive coverage in the European newspapers. Of course, entrepreneurs were quick to capitalize on the situation. Within a few years of the war the town sported several hotels and cafés. For some reason of fate, at Rue Flamanville 51 the name *Aux Ruines de Bazeilles* is still just about legible below the top floor windows. The café was opened in 1871 and changed hands several times before it was finally turned into a private home.

Continue for another 300 metres until you are at the site of **Villa Beurmann (14)** (N49°40.841′ E004°58.598′). The villa had been changed into a fortress by the French and occupied a key position in preventing the Germans from reaching Sedan. On the afternoon of 1 September the situation for the men of 3rd Marine Infantry Regiment quickly deteriorated and the few surviving officers fled to the Taverne Bourgerie, where they prepared themselves for the now famous last stand.

Walk along the D764 for another 150 metres until you are back at the museum.

REMINDER: *If you have borrowed the key of the Ossuary, do not forget to return it. If the museum has closed, put it in the mailbox.*

Villa Beurmann in 2019.

Walk 3

Floing

Duration: half a day's tour
Distance: 10 kilometres
Map: IGN 3009 E Sedan

This circular walk starts at St. Charles' Cemetery in Sedan (N49°42.629′ E004°56.393′). It is designed to retrace the steps of the last French cavalry charge of 1870 and its commander, General Marguerite. The cemetery can be reached via the D5 that runs from Sedan city centre to Floing, see map Walk 3. There is a parking space on the left of the cemetery entrance, next to the Jewish Cemetery. It is advisable to carry water. Sturdy shoes are recommended; the route of the walk follows farm tracks as well as tarmac. There are supermarkets, bakeries and restaurants in Sedan and Floing. Apart from in restaurants and cafés, there are no public toilets along the route. NOTE: the going is quite steep in some places; for this walk you need to be physically in good condition. The last few kilometres of the walk are downhill. It is also possible to do the tour by a car with sufficient ground clearance or by mountain bike.

GPS coordinates for Walk 3:

(1)	German 14-18 Monument	N49°42.700′ E004°56.528′)
(2)	1870 Monument and 1914-1918 Cemetery	(N49°42.719′ E004°56.528′)
(3)	Le Chêne Brisé	(N49°42.509′ E004°56.111′)
(4)	Grotte du Massacre 1944	(N49°42.658′ E004°55.698′)
(5)	Statue of General Marguerite	(N49°43.292′ E004°55.650′)
(6)	Floing 1870 Cemetery	(N49°43.153′ E004°55.826′)
(7)	Floing National War Cemetery	(N49°43.022′ E004°55.998′)
(8)	African Chasseurs Monument	(N49°43.176′ E004°56.076′)
(9)	Camille de Varaigne Monument	(N49°43.008′ E004°56.078′)
(10)	General Marguerite Monument	(N49°43.206′ E004°56.518′)
(11)	Weimar Monument	(N49°43.223′ E004°56.585′)
(12)	Taverne le Terme	(N49°43.230′ E004°56.605′)

Saint-Menges

German
Guns

Illy

D205

D6

D5

D5

X

D205

Floing

D205

11 12

5

8

Le Terme
Wood

Garenne
Wood

7

10

6

9

N

500 m
- - -..- - Tracks

©Bart Metselaar

4

1

3

2

SEDAN

D5

Balan

Park your car in the parking space on the left of the entrance of **St.
Charles' Communal Cemetery**. (N49°42.629′ E004°56.393′). Once
within the cemetery walls you can conveniently follow the sign
'Monument Allemand'. Even without signs, the **German 1914-1918
Monument (1)** N49°42.700′ E004°56.528′) is not easy to ignore: it is a
large, temple-like building, located left-centre of the cemetery's central
lane. Soon after the German occupation of Sedan on 25-26 August 1914,

The German monument in St. Charles Communal Cemetery, Sedan, in 1916 and 2016.

they started to bury their dead in St. Charles' Cemetery. There were several military hospitals in Sedan and therefore a substantial cemetery was needed. Not wasting time, the Germans started building walls in the middle of the communal cemetery to fence off theirs. Today these walls have disappeared. Much later it was decided that a central monument was needed to honour the fallen. The Brandenburg Gate like structure, made from reinforced concrete, was built between June and October 1915. The resemblance with the famous Brandenburg Gate in Berlin was entirely intentional. The generation of men who were part of the German Army in 1914 were brought up with patriotic ceremonies associated with *Sedantag*, Sedan Day. Naturally, the main festivities of 2 September, the day of Napoleon's capitulation, took place in Berlin at the Brandenburg Gate. Apparently, even forty-five years after Napoleon's defeat, the Germans could not resist rubbing the reality of the defeat into the French noses.

In the 1920s the bodies in the German cemetery were exhumed and reburied in the large German concentration cemetery of Noyers-Pont-Maugis, some five kilometres south of Sedan. In 1937 the Sedan city council decided to demolish the walls but to preserve the monument. During the Second World War the Wehrmacht used the cemetery again. After that war the bodies were again transferred to Noyers. In later years the condition of the building deteriorated, but no one felt responsible and certainly not responsible enough to pay for urgently necessary repairs. From 2005 until 2017 the monument was fenced off as it was slowly falling apart and had become a hazard. In 2011 there were plans to tear the whole thing down. After years of protest, even from abroad, to preserve the monument, the City Council of Sedan reluctantly took on responsibility and started the restoration of this unique monument, receiving financial support from German and French authorities. Today, after 104 years of neglect, the monument has now been justly restored to its former glory.

Return to the central lane. The **1870 Monument and 1914-1918 Cemetery (2)** (N49°42.719′ E004°56.528′) are located at the far end of the central lane. The design of the French 1870 monument is, as in most cemeteries, of the obelisk type. It marks the spot of a French mass grave. A little behind the monument is the St. Charles Necropole Nationale. This cemetery is dedicated to French soldiers who died during the First World War. However, it also holds British, Russian and Romanian graves. These soldiers all died as German prisoners of war. (Russian

The French 1870 monument in St. Charles.

and Romanian prisoners were often used as forced labourers.) There are also dozens of Belgian civilian graves. They all died from various acts of war. In total, 1,489 people are buried here.

Return to the entrance of the cemetery and walk downhill along the Rue de Cimetière. After about fifty metres take the right fork; you are now walking along the Bvd (Boulevard) des 147eme et 347eme Regiment. If you look to the right, you will see the remains of the walls of the Sedan Citadel. Turn right at the crossroads; you are now walking along the D5. After twenty metres you arrive at **Le Chêne Brisé (3)** (N49°42.509' E004°56.111'), the Broken Oak Monument. Here, an unknown – but according to some sources 'a significant number' – of combatants killed during the last hours of the battle are buried.

25. — *Sedan.* - Le Chêne brisé, sépulture de soldats français (1870).

A postcard of the Chêne Brisé dating from 1910; note the absence of arm and hammer.

The Grotte du Massacre 1944.

The monument represents an oak (one of the symbols of Sedan) that is coming back to life and a woman who is trying to destroy a gun with a sledge hammer. The hammer has long since disappeared, as well as various other elements of the sculpture. Despite missing these parts, the monument remains a protest against war and yet one of hope for the future. The inhabitants of Floing raised the funds, after which local marble sculptor Constant Duc was commissioned to make the work.

Cross the street and continue along the D5 in the direction of Floing. After 600 metres you will see **Grotte du Massacre 1944 (4)** (N49°42.658′ E004°55.698′) across the street. On 22 August 1944, only a few weeks before the Americans liberated Sedan (6 September 1944), a group of French Nazis fled towards Germany. On 28 August this group of fanatics managed to lure a group of French resistance fighters into a trap. Nine were killed and one, though wounded, managed to escape. The killing continued the next day. In a rage of madness and sadism, eleven people were locked up in the cave, 'interrogated', tortured and, finally, shot in the neck. To finish off anyone still breathing, the French Nazis fired several bursts of sub-machine gun bullets into the helpless people. Miraculously, one man survived the killing by pretending to be dead. The sole survivor of the massacre, Georges Cablat, not unsurprisingly, never recovered from the tragedy.

After another 1,500 metres along the D5 you will arrive at the town centre of Floing. On the left side of the road there is a **Statue of General**

General Marguerite, 1823-1870.

Statue of General Marguerite in Floing.

Marguerite (5) (N49°43.292′ E004°55.650′). Born in 1823 in the Meuse, Marguerite was a brilliant cavalry officer who rose quickly through the ranks. He spent a lot of time abroad, serving as a regimental commander in Algeria, arguably France's most important colony. Called back to France in August 1870, he was quickly appointed a major general and took over command of the Second Reserve Cavalry Division. He enjoyed his new status for only eight days; he died of wounds on 6 September 1870, four days after the capitulation of Sedan. In 1887 a statue was unveiled in Kouba, Algeria, where he had been stationed for many years. When in 1968, after a horrible war (1954-1962), Algeria became an independent country, the statue was returned to France and ultimately placed at the heart of the village.

On the afternoon of 1 September 1870, at the summit of the fighting around Sedan, the Germans had already taken Floing and were now working their way up hill to attack the Floing Heights. (Facing the Marguerite statue, the heights are on your left.) Strategically, the loss of the Floing Heights would mean the loss of Sedan. Trying to stem the tide, General Ducrot ordered General Marguerite to advance across the Floing Heights and remove the Germans from the hill. This meant advancing

162

along a barren ridge without cover and in full sight of the German guns that were located only a kilometre away. Marguerite set out to reconnoitre the terrain but was immediately hit by a bullet that smashed his jaw and blew out his teeth. General Galliffet was ordered to take his place. Soon afterwards, about 1,800 men started crossing the heights but were met with devastating artillery fire. Almost one thousand French cavalry men died during the charge. The rest of the tour is dedicated to the charge and the monuments on the Floing Heights.

Cross the D5 and follow the signs (opposite the Mairie, the town hall) 'Memorial des Chasseurs d'Afrique', D205, Illy and Givonne. After about fifty metres take the first road on the right and walk uphill toward the church; follow the road around the church and keep right. After about 200 metres you will arrive at **Floing 1870 Cemetery (6)** (N49°43.153′ E004°55.826′). This cemetery is in fact a mass grave; the headstones are dedicated to regiments, officers, etc. The bodies buried here were mainly found in the village centre of Floing; it is estimated that there are between 2,000 and 3,000 bodies in the grave, but there could be more. The carnage was such that it is not surprising that even today bodies are still occasionally found. Rusted guns, bayonets, bombs and the remains of horses are relatively common finds here.

There is an interesting memorial plaque attached to the wall on the left. Believed to be buried in this cemetery is military veterinarian Pierre Constant Louis Chauvin. The lack of doctors and nurses to take

Pierre Constant Louis CHAUVIN
Vétérinaire
Nè le 13.2.1825
Mort le 16.9.1870
par suite de Blessures Reçues
le 1.9.1870 à la Bataille
de SEDAN

Floing 1870 Cemetery.

care of the overwhelming number of wounded was such that anyone who was deemed suitable for the job was pressed into service. Chauvin had been working for all hours since 29 August. On the afternoon of 1 September, with bullets and shrapnel flying everywhere, Chauvin was hit while dressing wounds in Floing. He died fifteen days later.

Leave the cemetery and turn right. Follow the road, the Rue des Brave Gens (Street of Brave Men), for about 500 metres uphill. While following the battle through his binoculars, King Wilhelm I of Prussia reportedly shouted, 'Oh, the brave men!' when he saw the African cavalry charging through a hail of exploding shells. When you reach the top, the French **Floing National War Cemetery (7)** (N49°43.022′ E004°55.998′) is right in front of you. This cemetery is another sad proof of the chequered history of the French border region. On the summit of the Floing Heights, or the Terme Plateau, you will find monuments of three different wars that shaped European history: 1870-1871, 1914-1918 and 1939-1945. The Floing National War Cemetery is the last resting place of 2,237 victims of the First and Second World War. Starting in 1960, dozens of small local cemeteries from the area around Sedan were concentrated here. In this cemetery there are buried 2,957 French soldiers, including two Serbs, a Spaniard and several other members of the French resistance who were executed by the Germans during the Second World War; the Great War plot holds 333 graves.

Floing National War Cemetery; this is the plot dedicated to colonial troops.

African Cavalry Memorial park.

The African Cavalry Monument.

Leave the cemetery, turn left and walk for a hundred metres uphill. At the end of the road you will see the **African Chasseurs Monument (8)** (N49°43.176′ E004°56.076′). Marguerite's cavalry division was entirely made up from Colonial, African regiments. The memorial, dedicated to the twelve regiments that participated in the charge, was made by sculpture Emile Guillaume and was inaugurated on 1 September 1910, exactly forty years after the battle. It was financed by gifts under the patronage of the African Cavalry Veterans' Organization.

ICI REPOSENT
LE L'-COLONEL DE LINIERS CDT LE 3ᵉ REGIMENT DE CHASSEURS D'AFRIQUE
ET 150 SOUS-OFFICIERS BRIGADIERS ET CHASSEURS DES 1ᵉ 3ᵉ ET 4ᵉ REGIMENTS DE CHASSEURS D'AFRIQUE
MORTS POUR LA FRANCE
PENDANT LES CHARGES DE LA DIVISION MARGUERITTE LE 1ᵉʳ SEPT 1870
FLOING LE 24 SEPTEMBRE 1950

Mass grave monument of Lieutenant Colonel Liniers and 150 African cavalrymen.

At ground level, to the left of the principal monument, there is a square, roof-like structure. This is the mass grave of Lieutenant Colonel de Liniers, commander of the 3rd African Cavalry, and his troops. In 1950, de Liniers and 150 officers and horsemen were found at the base of a very old oak tree near Taverne le Terme. It was quickly decided that they should be reburied within the boundaries of the African Chasseurs Monument. The tombstone was unveiled on 24 September 1950. The whole site was renovated and provided with information panels by Souvenir Français in 2005.

Leave the cemetery and turn left. After 150 metres (it is signposted), take a right turn and continue for 350 metres down hill along the farm track until you come to the grave of Captain **Camille de Varaigne du Bourg (9)** (N49°43.008′ E004°56.78′). The site is marked by a lone

Lieutenant Colonel Liniers.

Signpost to Varaigne's grave.

tree. Varaigne du Bourg is buried where he was killed. Varaigne du Bourg was an officer of the 3rd African Cavalry Regiment and served under Colonel Clicquot, who was also killed during the charge. In total, two generals (Marguerite and Tilliard), seventy officers and a thousand cavalrymen lost their lives.

Walk back to the road and turn right. After about a hundred metres you will see a high voltage pylon in the field on your left. When you are at the same alignment as the pylon, take a look at the panoramic photograph in the book.

Grave of Captain Varaigne.

German guns

Garenne Wood

The Marguerite Memorial

The Floing Heights

Panorama of the Terme Plateau looking north-east.

By now the French Army was in deep trouble. Once the German artillery had managed to destroy the French gun batteries on the Terme Plateau, the net around Sedan tightened. At around 2.00 pm Saxon infantry regiments started to climb the northern hillside (from the general direction where the pylon stands, see panoramic photo). In order to stop the enemy from taking the plateau and consequently the last line of defence before Sedan, Marguerite's cavalry division was thrown in the fray.

Continue for another fifty metres, until you see the **General Marguerite Monument (10)** (N49°43.206′ E004°56.518′) on the right side of the road. Marguerite was struck about fifty metres behind the monument. After the third check on the German positions, Marguerite was shot through the face and evacuated from the

Marguerite monument.

Romanticized painting of the wounded General Marguerite by J.A. Walker.

battlefield. He was succeeded by General de Galliffet, who immediately set out to avenge Marguerite. (In spite of this, the charge became famous as Marguerite's last cavalry charge.) Initially the charge seemed to bear fruit as the German infantry started to retreat downhill. This, however, was only done to create a clear field of fire for the German guns on Hatois Hill, see the panoramic photograph. The carnage that followed defies any description. Soon after the barrage started the hillside was covered with dead horses and men. When the French spearheads turned 180 degrees and hurried back to Garenne Wood they were fired upon by their own infantry, who were under the impression that the Germans had launched a counter attack. Meanwhile, fresh French cavalry were still leaving Garenne Wood on their way to Floing, adding to the mayhem. At 4.15 pm it was all over for the French and the Prussians prepared to press on to Sedan. Against all odds, Major Cugnon d'Alincourt and sixty cavalrymen, swords drawn, launched a final attack. They were shot to pieces. By sheer luck, General de Galliffet survived the carnage and was taken prisoner. After the war ended he returned to army command, taking a notable and controversial part in the suppression of the Paris Commune, went on to rise to high rank and became a minister for war. He died in 1909.

Nowadays there are patches of wood spread across the plateau; in 1870 it was a barren ridge that was exclusively used for growing crops and consequently offered an unobstructed view for the German gunners.

General de Galliffet, 1830-1909.

Not far from Marguerite's monument stands the **Weimar Monument (11)** (N49°43.223′ E004°56.585′). The monument was erected by veterans of the 94th Infantry Regiment from Weimar, a German city 300 kilometres south of Berlin and birth place of Goethe (1749-1832). Prince Albert of Saxony (1828-1902) commanded a Saxon army 120,000 strong. He was tasked with completing the encirclement of Sedan from the east and the north. When Marguerite's cavalry charge started the Saxons were preparing an attack east of Garenne Wood,

Prince Albert of Saxony, 1828-1902.

effectively completing the encirclement of Sedan and cutting off Marguerite's retreat. At 4.30, the Saxons eliminated the last French pockets of resistance. When the northern and eastern defences collapsed, thousands of panic-stricken soldiers fled to Sedan, flooding the already overcrowded city. Not long thereafter Napoleon III surrendered. About fifty metres past the Weimar Monument stands a lone house. This is the **Taverne Le Terme (12)** (N49°43.230′ E004°56.605′). Over the last one and a half century some alterations have been made, but it is basically the same building. In 1950, close to

The Saxon Weimar Monument.

169

Taverne Le Terme today (2019).

Shell fragment in the field opposite Le Terme.

the Taverne, the bodies of Lieutenant Colonel Liniers and 150 other ranks were found. Marguerite received first aid here before he was evacuated from the battlefield.

From this point the tarmac road ends and changes into a farm track. Follow the track for a kilometre until you are on the edge of Garenne Wood, where Marguerite and his cavalry assembled before they started the charge on Floing. Turn right onto the Voie de Garenne (indicated by a signpost that reads: 'La Garenne, 1,4 km'), and walk down hill. After a kilometre you come to a T-junction; turn right onto the Avenue André Payer, a rather grandiose name for what is a farm track. After two kilometres, when you return to a more urban world, turn left. This narrow and winding street is the Ruelle Servais. At the end of this Ruelle turn left; you are now back at the Rue de Cimetière.

Car Tour 2

Sedan and surroundings

Duration: a full day's tour
Distance: 30 kilometres
Map: IGN 3009 E Sedan

This circular tour starts and ends in Sedan at the Monument aux Morts 1870, situated on the Place d'Alsace-Lorraine (N49°41.962′ E004°57.096′) at the junction of the D8043A and the D5 in Sedan. The tour takes the visitor along the heavily contested ravine of the Givonne Creek, where the Germans smashed through the French lines. Also covered are the hills surrounding Sedan from the north and east from which General Marguerite launched his legendary last cavalry attack.

Most of the route is along tarmac roads and is easy accessible. However, the narrow roads off the main road leading to the cemeteries at Daigny and Givonne are not suitable for vehicles larger than camper vans and minibuses. This does not necessarily have to be a major problem as the cemeteries can be easily reached by a short walk (fifty metres) from the main road. Bars, restaurants shops and bakeries can be found in Balan, Givonne and Sedan. Generally speaking, restaurants are open between 12.00 and 2.00 pm, and from 7.00 pm. There is a petrol station along the D8043A, between the D17 and the N43, see map Car Tour 2.

GPS coordinates for Car Tour 2:

(1) Sedan Monument aux Morts 1870   (N49°41.962′ E004°57.096′)
(2) Balan Mass Grave   (N49°41.436′ E004°58.027′)
(3) Balan Civilian Monument   (N49°41.401′ E004°57.997′)
(4) Croix d'Hendecourt Monument   (N49°41.330′ E004°58.687′)
(5) Croix MacMahon Monument   (N49°41.309′ E004°58.791′)
(6) La Moncelle French Mass Grave   (N49°41.277′ E004°59.389′)
(7) Grave of Beulwitz, Barth and Schmidt (N49°41.276′ E004°59.386′)
(8) Grave of Lehning and Heydemann   (N49°41.272′ E004°59.409′)
(9) Daigny Mass Grave Monument   (N49°42.093′ E004°59.563′)

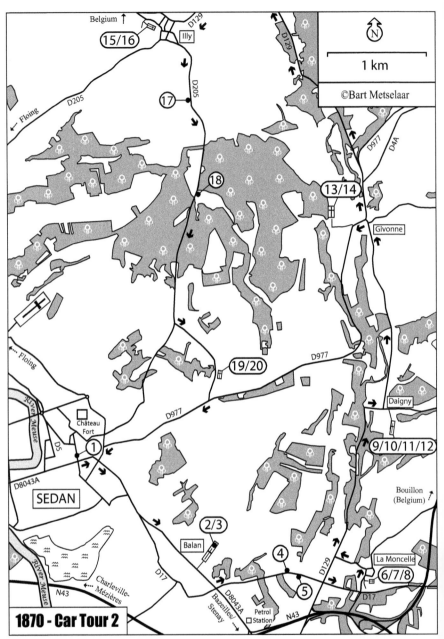

(10) Otto von Maerk crucifix   (N49°42.085′ E004°59.565′)
(11) Graves of Steinmayer and Altrock   (N49°42.081′ E004°59.563′)
(12) Grave of Heinrich von Schoenberg   (N49°42.079′ E004°59.565′)
(13) Graves of Hans von Alvensleben,
       Joppen and Schulze   (N49°43.197′ E004°59.063′)

(14) Givonne mass grave monument	(N49°43.204′ E004°59.064′)
(15) Carré Militaire	(N49°44.143′ E004°57.577′)
(16) Grave of Captain Fleury Verna	(N49°44.145′ E004°57.575′)
(17) Calvaire d'Illy	(N49°43.802′ E004°57.872′)
(18) Garenne Farm and Garenne Wood	(N49°43.256′ E004°57.899′)
(19) Tabatière Cemetery	(N49°42.360′ E004°58.130′)
(20) Graves of Davis and Tiedemann	(N49°42.358′ E004°58.123′)

You can park your car on the left or right of the **Monument aux Morts 1870 (1)** (N49°41.962′ E004°57.096′). If you are in need of supplies, there is a bakery/patisserie about fifty metres behind the monument.

After the defeat of Sedan, it had become painfully clear that the formidable but now obsolete fortifications were no match for modern artillery. As a consequence, between 1877 and 1884 most of the citadel of Sedan was demolished to make room for a redevelopment project. Consequently there is not much left of the fortifications. Fortunately, Sedan Castle, started in 1424 and with successive additions the largest late medieval fortress in Europe, was spared. New wide roads and streets were built and at the centre of the new city precinct a large town square was planned. The city council of Sedan though it appropriate to commemorate the victims of the 1870 War, by then

Sedan Monument aux Morts 1870.

inextricably linked to Sedan, by a large monument on the newly built square. The monument was built between 1894 and 1897 and was paid for by national subscription. The bronze bas-reliefs depict the battles of Bazailles and Floing. Both the bas-reliefs and the bronze statues were made by local sculptor Aristide Croisy.

Take the D8043A, direction Balan. After about 500 metres you will find a large First World War Monument in front of you; here the road makes a sharp bend to the left. Stay on the D8043A for another 1.5 kilometres until you see a life size, white crucifix on the right side of the

The Balan mass grave monument.

crossroads. Here, take a left turn into the (tiny) Rue du Cimetière. After fifty metres you can park your car in the parking space on your left, adjacent to the cemetery. Once inside the cemetery you will see the large crucifix of the **Balan Mass Grave (2)** (N49°41.436′ E004°58.027′) on your left. The memorial is enclosed by a brick wall and has a beautifully designed wrought iron gate. It commemorates 228 French and 613 German soldiers and eight civilians, of whom one is a woman. The marble plaque claims that all the bodies are buried on this spot but it is much more likely that such a large number of bodies are buried somewhere outside the perimeter of the cemetery. Interestingly, a bronze plaque is dedicated to Charles Durand, *franc-tireur,* a civilian who joined the French army to fight against the Bavarians. Wounded on 1 September, he died on 15 September. Interestingly the donor of the plaque is almost identified, for at the bottom of the plaque is inscribed: *'son ami, E. de V.'* (his friend E. de V.).

Facing the gate of the Balan memorial, the **Balan Civilian Monument (3)** (N49°41.401′ E004°57.997′) is on your left. Unfortunately, at the time of writing not much information could be found about this memorial that commemorates twenty-two civilians, including four children, who were killed on 1 September 1870. Whether they are buried in the cemetery or just remembered here remains unknown.

Continue on the D8043A for another hundred metres in the direction

Balan monument to the civilian victims of 1870.

of Bazeilles. At the traffic lights, take a left turn onto the D17, direction La Moncelle. This street is appropriately called Rue General MacMahon. After about 700 metres, stop at the **Croix d'Hendecourt Monument (4)** (N49°41.330′ E004°58.687′), situated behind a low hedge on the left side of the road opposite the 'Balan' sign. Be careful when you get out of your car; this is a very busy and narrow road.

Croix d'Hendecourt Monument.

On 1 September, at 6.00 am, in an ultimate attempt to seek glory and possibly death by leading his troops on the battlefield, Napoleon left Sedan on horseback to reconnoitre the situation at Bazailles. He was accompanied by two of his personal staff officers. Upon reaching Balan (the area close to the cemetery) they found themselves amidst heavy fighting. Continuing along the modern-day D17 they were surprised by a German artillery barrage in which Staff Captain Louis Lesergeant d'Hendecourt was killed and the other (unknown) officer wounded. Napoleon escaped the inferno unscathed and continued to La Moncelle and Givonne, where he defied death a second time. Utterly depressed with what he had seen on the battlefield and in excruciating pains because of his chronic bladder stone, he returned to Sedan, where he safely arrived at 11.00 am. The memorial to Staff Captain d'Hendecourt is erected on the approximate spot where he was killed.

Return to your car and continue for a hundred metres. Opposite the white house on the left stands the **Croix MacMahon Monument (5)** (N49°41.309′ E004°58.791′), built on the right

Croix MacMahon.

bank of what is now the driveway of a house. You can park (briefly!) on the driveway. Note the 1920s cast iron Rue du Maréchal de Mac Mahon road sign.

The battle for Sedan started at 4.00 am, when the Bavarians launched the attack on Bazailles. At 5.45 am, Marshal MacMahon arrived at this vantage point, called the Rapaille Heights, to observe the French and German positions around Sedan. At around 6.00 am, a shell fired from Pont Maugis exploded on MacMahon's position, seriously wounding the Army Commander. When he was evacuated, he passed out due to the loss of blood but not before preparing a message that appointed General Ducrot, Commander of I Corps, the new head of the Army of Châlons. The orders arrived at Ducrot's HQ at about 7.30 am, adding to the chaos in the French army.

Continue along the D17 to La Moncelle. At the crossroads, go straight ahead. On entering the village, take the second T-junction on the left; the first one is a one-way street. Follow this road for about 100 metres and follow the sign 'Eglise', Church. Take a 180° turn into the Rue d'Eglise and park in front of the church (N49°41.273′ E004°59.344′). The cemetery can be reached by a path on the right side of the church. Once there, the obelisk of the **French Mass Grave (6)** (N49°41.277′ E004°59.389′) is on your left. The monument commemorates 300 French soldiers who were killed on 1 September while they were desperately holding on to their positions against an overwhelming enemy. The monument was inaugurated on 5 September 1909.

The La Moncelle French Mass Grave Monument.

To the left of the French monument lies the headstone of **Wilhelm von Beulwitz, Julius Barth and Julius Schmidt (7)** (N49°41.276′ E004°59.386′). First Lieutenant Von Beulwitz, Corporal Barth and Private Schmidt, 1st Company of the 107th Royal Saxon Infantry Regiment, were killed on 1 September by the infamous French machine guns. Their relatives paid for the monument in memory of their loved ones. The 107th Regiment was part of the XII Royal Saxon Army Corps, commanded by Crown Prince Albert of Saxony. Unfortunately, no further details could be found, neither on line nor in the literature. At the far end of the cemetery are the German grave markers of **Captain Joseph Lehning and Lieutenant Carl Heydemann (8)** (N49°41.272′ E004°59.409′) of the Bavarian 12th Infantry Regiment. Again, no additional information could be found.

Grave of Beulwitz, Barth and Schmidt.

Drive back to the crossroads D17/D129 and turn right onto the D129 in the direction of Daigny. At the modern church, follow the sign 'Cimetière', continue straight ahead and take the second road to the right. After fifty metres, you will arrive at Daigny Communal Cemetery. Park your car here. Walk along the cemetery wall to the entrance and climb the stairs. The **1870 Monument (9)** (N49°42.093′ E004°59.563′) is to your immediate right. After the

Grave of Lehning and Heydemann.

Daigny mass grave monument.

battle dozens of bodies were delivered at the cemetery on improvised stretchers by locals. To dispose of the decaying corpses, which were often missing limbs and showing large impact wounds from lead bullets, large pits were dug. A horrible side effect of lead bullets

is that they partly disintegrate when hitting bone, like a hollow point bullet or dum

The difference in the size of bullets: left 1914, right 1870.

dum. It is not clear where the mass graves are situated. Interestingly, the 1870 monument in Daigny makes no mention of the nationality of the dead, nor does it bear the usual *Mort pour la France* inscription. Therefore, it is most likely that it remembers both French and German casualties.

Take a right turn on the central path; after thirty metres, on your left, you will see the crucifix of **Otto von Maerk (10)** (N49°42.085′ E004°59.565′). Maerk was a sergeant in the 2nd Saxon Jäger Battalion No. 15. Nothing could be found about Maerk and the beautifully cast iron crucifix; in fact, it is not even certain if his last name really is

Otto von Maerk crucifix.

179

Graves of Steinmayer and Altrock.

Maerk as the name is hardly legible on the monument. Return to the central path; after thirty metres you will come to the headstones of **Steinmayer and Altrock (11)** (N49°42.081′ E004°59.563′). Both monuments are heavily weathered and it is very hard to see what the engravings are. The headstone on the left reads: *'Offizierskorps des dritten Inf. Reg. Prinz Carl von Baiern* [sic]. *Dem gefallen Kameraden Hauptmann Joseph Steinmayer und Lieutnant Georg Heind. Zum Andenken gewidmet, Sedan den 1ᵉⁿ September 1870.'*

The headstone on the right reads: *'Hier ruhen im Glauben in ein der einstiges Wiedersehen Paul Wilhelm von Altrock, Second Lieutnant in Konigl. Saechs. Grenadier Regiment Konig Wilhelm von Preussen No 1, geboren zu Glauschnitt am 12. April 1849, und Ludwig Battmann, Vice Feldwebel in demselbsten Regiment, geboren im Grossenhain am 13. September 1846. Beide in der Schlacht bei Sedan am 1ᵉⁿ September 1870 gevallen. Selig sind die in dem Herrn sterben etc.'* The grave of **Heinrich von Schoenberg (12)** (N49°42.079′ E004°59.565′), marked by a beautiful cast iron Maltese Cross, is situated in the same row, a few metres further along from the other two. Von Schoenberg, born into the noble House of Bornitz on 16 August 1848, was a lieutenant in the 13th Jäger Battalion of Saxony; he was killed during the fighting in La Moncelle. Schoenberg was the recipient of the Military Order of St. Heinrich, a military order of the Kingdom of Saxony and the oldest military order of the states of the German Empire.

Return to your car and drive back to the main road. At the crossroads, take a right turn onto the D129, direction Givonne. The barrel of the French tank in the town square points you in the right direction. After two kilometres you enter Givonne, a small rural town at the bottom of the

Grave of Heinrich von Schoenberg.

Givonne Valley. Take a left at the main T-junction and leave the main road, the D977, after just fifty metres. Continue straight up the hill and follow the sign 'Cimetière' along the Voie Royale, a rather grand name for a tiny country road. The second road on the right leads you to the cemetery; you can park your car to the left of the entrance gate.

The grave monument of Second Lieutenant **Hans von Alvensleben,** Sergeant **Wilhelm Joppen** and Sergeant **Georg Schulze (13)** (N49°43.197′ E004°59.063′) are situated on the left side of the main path. Interestingly, there are two more names at the bottom of the monument, namely Second Lieutenant Peter von Henning und Schönhoff and Second Lieutenant von Kirchbach. Both second lieutenants are buried *'in ihrer Heimat',* in their home country, but are remembered on this monument. They all have in common the fact that they were part of the Prussian Garde Fusilier Regiment, an infantry unit of the Guards Corps of the Prussian Army, garrisoned in Berlin. In keeping with the genteel

181

Graves of Hans von Alvensleben, Joppen and Schulze.

The Givonne Mass Grave Monument.

nature of the unit, most of its officer corps were nobility. As you might have noticed, most of the individual 1870 memorials are dedicated to officers of noble families.

To the right of the 1870 grave monument lies the rectangular plot of the **Givonne Mass Grave Monument (14)** (N49°43.204′ E004°59.064′). The ridge between Givonne and Daigny were the last defences on Sedan's right flank. The Saxon and Bavarian regiments launched heavy attacks on both villages and quickly seized several bridges across the River Givonne. Not many details could be found about the monument other than that there are 924 French and German soldiers buried here.

Return to the main road and drive back to the T-junction in Givonne's centre. Take a left onto the D129 and follow this road to Illy, direction La Chapelle. Once in Illy, leave the D129, take a left turn onto the D205 and take a right turn just before you reach the church. You can park in front of the Mairie. Facing the Mairie, go left; when you reach the fence (of a playground) go right. The cemetery lies right in front of you. Immediately after you enter the cemetery you will find the **Carré Militaire (15)** (N49°44.143′ E004°57.577′) on the left. It holds the French memorials of Gravier, Noel and Minary. Now that Daigny and Givonne had fallen into enemy hands, the Germans mounted increasing pressure on Illy, the other key to the Floing Heights. If Illy could be taken, the Floing Heights would be the only French defences before Sedan; victory was within the Germans'

Lieutenant Paul-Jean Gravier, Vicomte de Vergennes, Chasseurs d'Afrique.

Lieutenant Léon Evariste Noel, Hussards.

Commander Minary, Zouaves.

grasp. The three French officers that are buried here are from three different units, Chasseurs d'Afrique, Hussards (a type of cavalry regiment) and Zouaves (light infantry). Amongst these is the grave of Paul Jean Gravier, Vicomte de Vergennes, killed on 1 September. An ancestor had been largely responsible, as French Foreign Secretary, for the French intervention in the American War of Independence. These were the sad remains of the French army that were by now desperately trying to keep the Germans from taking Illy. Adjacent to the 1870 memorials lies a plot dedicated to French soldiers of the Great War.

The grave of **Fleury Vernay (16)** (N49°44.145′ E004°57.575′) is on the other side of the main path. Vernay, an artillery captain, was wounded on 1 September but

Grave of Captain Fleury Vernay.

Calvaire d'ILLY
La Croix à gauche du Calvaire indique l'endroit où le Général Margueritte fut blessé, et le point de départ
G. Bontillot, édit. Sedan de la dernière charge des chasseurs d'Afrique

Calvaire d'Illy in about 1900.

died four days later, aged only forty. Sadly, his grave marker is in a rather derelict state.

Return to your vehicle, turn around and take a right on the D205. At the T-junction, take the left fork, direction *Sedan par fond de Givonne*. Stay on the D205 and follow the sign *Calvaire* (Calvary). After a kilometre you will arrive at the site of the **Calvaire d'Illy (17)** (N49°43.802′ E004°57.872′). You can park your car on the country road on the right of the D205. The site is also known by the name Croix Margueritte, after General Margueritte, who assembled his troops here in the beginning of the afternoon for what has become famed as France's last major cavalry charge.

The 3rd African Cavalry, commanded by Lieutenant Colonel de Liniers, was in support of

Lieutenant Colonel de Liniers.

Garenne

SEDAN
(behind hill)

F

French Cavalry Attack

Marguerite's right flank. While rallying his troops, Liniers was shot through the hand but continued issuing orders. While leading the attack on Floing Heights, he was shot through the hip. Quickly, he was taken to the only shelter on the battlefield, the Taverne le Terme. By this time, the air was so thick with shrapnel and bullets that Liniers was hit a third time; he was killed instantly. His body was only accidentally found in 1950 during a landscaping project. He was exhumed and reburied, along with 150 men that were also buried in this mass grave, within the boundaries of the African Chasseurs Memorial (see Floing, Walk 3, Stop 8).

Walk back to your car and continue along the country road until you are at the highest point, close to the high voltage pylon. From here, with the aid of the panoramic photograph in the book, you have a clear view across the battlefield.

Stay on the D205. After one kilometre, on entering Garenne Woods, **Garenne Farm (18)** (N49°43.256′ E004°57.899′) is on your left. The red and white communication mast is a very useful landmark as it roughly marks the spot from where part of the French cavalry massed in preparation for the attack on Floing. Garenne Farm was used as a French HQ and forward hospital.

Garenne Farm.

Panorama Floing Heights.

Tabatière Communal Cemetery.

Continue along the D205 for a kilometre. At the T-junction take the left fork; there are sport fields on your right hand side. After passing a cemetery on your right, continue for another kilometre. **Tabatière Cemetery** lies on the left of the road. There is no parking space in front of the cemetery, but as long as you are not blocking the entrance to the driveway on your right you can (briefly) park here. Three **German grave monuments (19)** (N49°42.360′ E004°58.130′) are erected on the right side of the main path; the one in the middle has the characteristic green 1873 cast iron fence built around it.

The grave on the left is that of Constance von Twardovski. Born on 26 September 1836, he was the former consul in Constantinople.

Front row, left: Twardovski; centre: Schultz, Cammerer and Quint; right: Oscar von Gössnitz. Second row, behind the Goulden family plot: left: James Davis, right: (obelisk type) Leo von Tiedemann.

Wounded on 1 September, he died on 5 September 1870 in La Moncelle. Next to Twardovski's grave is that of Eberhard Schultz, Hermann Cammerer II and Daniel Quint. Unfortunately, no additional information could be found about them. The grave monument on the right is that of Captain Oscar von Gössnitz, born on 15 February 1828, of the 6th Prussian Grenadier Regiment.

Up the stairs, immediately to the right, are the graves of **James Davis and Leo von Tiedemann (20)** (N49°42.358′ E004°58.123′). The one on the left is that of Christopher James Davis, a British-Barbadian physician. Davis was born in Bridgetown, Barbados, one of ten children.

Christopher James Davis. (1842-1870)

Educated in Europe and a doctor at St. Bart's Hospital in London, he wanted to help sick and injured during the Franco-Prussian war. He volunteered his services to assist the suffering and cholera-stricken peasantry of eastern France, especially at the Battle of Sedan. He devoted himself with skill and energy to the treatment of large numbers of both French and German sick and wounded and to the establishment of soup kitchens. Davis survived the war, but when he returned in an exhausted condition from a short visit to England, where he had been to raise further funds to carry on his good work, he succumbed to small-pox. He died on 27 November, at the age of twenty-eight. Davis was given a military funeral, headed by the Mayor of Sedan and which was followed by troops of both armies.

Lieutenant Tiedemann, born on 21 August 1844 in Rusocxin, Danzig (today the capital of the Province of Danzig in Poland), was killed close to this cemetery. Between 1873 and 1880 he and the other German soldiers that are buried here were exhumed from their field graves and reburied in Tabatière Cemetery.

Return to your car and continue along the D205; after two kilometres you will have returned to your starting point, the 1870 Monument at the Place d'Alsace-Lorraine in Sedan.

Grave of Leo von Tiedemann.

Appendix 1

Order of Battle – The French Army

Army of the Rhine:

Commander in Chief:	Napoleon III / Marshal Bazaine
Imperial Guard:	General Bourbaki
I Corps:	Marshal MacMahon
II Corps:	General Frossard
III Corps:	Marshal Bazaine (later succeeded by General Decaen; after Decaen was killed he was replaced by Marshal Le Bœuf)
IV Corps:	General Ladmirault
V Corps:	General de Failly
VI Corps:	Marshal Canrobert
VII Corps:	General Douay

Army of Châlons:

Commander in Chief:	Marshal MacMahon, with Napoleon III in an advisory role.
Chief of Staff:	General Faure
Imperial Guard Corps:	General Bourbaki
I Corps:	General Ducrot
V Corps:	General de Failly, replaced by General De Wimpffen on 31 August.
VII Corps:	General Douay
XII Corps:	General Lebrun

The army also included 27,000 horses, 348 guns and 84 machine guns

Struck by French political enemies soon after his defeat at Sedan: 'Napoleon III the miserable, perjurer and traitor'. Note the pickelhaube helmet.

188

Appendix 2

Order of Battle – The German Army

Commander in Chief:	Wilhelm I King of Prussia
Chief of the General Staff:	General Helmuth von Moltke
Quarter-Master General:	Lieutnant General von Podbielski

First Army:	**General Karl Friedrich von Steinmetz** (later General von Manteuffel)
VII Army Corps (VII. Armeekorps) (Westphalia):	General Heinrich von Zastrow
VIII Army Corps (VIII. Armeekorps) (Rhine Provinces):	General August Karl von Goeben
I Army Corps (I. Armeekorps) (East Prussia):	Cavalry General Edwin Freiherr von Manteuffel
II Army Corps:	Cavalry General Prince Frederick Charles
Guards Corps:	General Prince August von Württemberg
III Army Corps: (Brandenburg):	Lieutenant General Constantin von Alvensleben
IV Army Corps (Saxon Provinces and Anhalt):	Lieutenant General Gustav von Alvensleben
IX Army Corps (Schleswig -Holstein and Hesse):	General Albrecht Gustav von Manstein
X Army Corps (Hanover, Oldenburg and Brunswick):	General Konstantin Bernhard von Voigts-Rhetz
XII. (Royal Saxon) Army Corps:	Crown Prince Albert of Saxony
5th Cavalry Division:	Lieutenant General Baron von Rheinbaben
6th Cavalry Division:	Lieutenant General H.S.H. Duke Wilhelm of Mecklenburg-Schwerin
II Army Corps (Pomerania):	General Eduard von Fransecky

Third Army:	Crown Prince Friedrich Wilhelm of Prussia
V Army Corps (Posen and Liegnitz):	Lieutenant General Hugo von Kirchbach
XI Army Corps (Hesse, Nassau, Saxe-Weimar):	Lieutenant General Julius von Bose
I Royal Bavarian Corps:	General Ludwig Freiherr von der Tann
II Royal Bavarian Corps:	General Jakob von Hartmann
Württemberg Corps Command:	Frederick Francis II, Grand Duke of Mecklenburg-Schwerin
VI Army Corps (Silesia):	Cavalry General Wilhelm Georg von Tümpling
2nd Cavalry Division:	Lieutenant General Count Stolberg-Wernigerode
Fourth Army (Army of the Meuse):	**Crown Prince Albert of Saxony**

German troops in the Citadel of Sedan, September 1870.

Appendix 3

Short Biographies of Napoleon III and of Wilhelm I

Napoleon III (1808-1873)

Charles Louis Napoleon Bonaparte was the son of Louis Bonaparte, King of Holland (1806-1810) and the nephew of Napoleon I. The death of Napoleon I's son in 1832, the Duke of Reichstadt, made him the head and hope of the dynasty. Napoleon III twice attempted to overthrow King Louis-Philippe I, in 1836 and 1840; after the last attempt he was sentenced to life imprisonment. He managed to escape in 1846 (he walked out of his prison in Ham dressed as a workman, carrying a large board on his shoulder, hiding his face) and fled to Britain. The 1848 revolution in France – there were revolts in a number of European countries in 1848; the year is known to history as the 'Year of Revolutions') – enabled him to return to France.

Louis Bonaparte, nephew of Napoleon I.

Taking advantage of the popularity and prestige linked to the name of his famous uncle, he was elected to the new Constituent Assembly. Then, on 10 December 1848, he became Prince President of the Second Republic, winning a crushing majority. The Second Republic lasted from 1848 to 1852. Napoleon

Napoleon Bonaparte, Prince-President of France, 1848-1852.

manoeuvred skilfully and let the Assembly fall into disrepute through its conservative measures. He then took centre stage as the defender of universal suffrage, which ensured his popularity with the people. On 2 December 1851, once the Assembly had rejected a constitutional change that if passed would have enabled the President to stand for re-election, Napoleon organized a *coup d'état* and faced only token resistance. This also happened to be the same day and month that Napoleon I proclaimed himself Emperor of France in 1804. The new January 1852 Constitution gave him full power and on 2 December of that same year he declared himself Emperor of France with the title of Napoleon III. In the early years the revised monarchy certainly had the feel of an autocratic monarchy, admittedly with a greater awareness of social trends than most governments since the end of the Napoleonic Wars.

The industrial revolution made sure that new prosperity reached France; for the working class, however, living conditions remained very difficult. In foreign policy, Napoleon III was quick to take up arms, first in the Crimean War (1854-1856), where the French fought alongside the British army, in principle to support the Ottoman Empire but in fact to protect France's own interests and to prevent Russian future dominance of the region. He then intervened in Italy in 1859, supporting Piedmont in its struggle against Austrian rule in Italy, with the aim of Italian Unification, and gaining a useful chunk of territory in Savoy and the resort town of Nice for his efforts (1859) to achieve Italian unity. In both cases these actions enhanced France's prestige and were sufficiently 'liberal' and 'progressive' so as to reflect well on Napoleon III.

Despite his popularity, at least in foreign affairs, he had to tackle unrest, particularly amongst the industrial working classes. To remain in power, he changed several laws and aimed at creating a more liberal, less autocratic and arbitrary regime. However, his positive record for foreign interventions suffered badly as a consequence of the disaster that was the Mexico Expedition (1862-1867). His enemies, ranging from the traditional royalists, the Bourbonists, to the more socially radical on the left, with a whole range of '-ists' in between, were waiting in line to get rid of the emperor. What he needed was a new, successful war to re-establish his reign firmly and to protect the dynasty. What has become known as the Franco-Prussian War was a military disaster without precedent and led directly to the downfall of the imperial regime. Napoleon, who was freed after the war, went into exile in Britain (Chislehurst) where he died on 9 January 1873.

Saint Michael's Abbey, Farnborough, Great Britain. (Coll. B. Metselaar)

The sarcophagus of Emperor Napoleon III of France. (Coll. B. Metselaar)

He is buried in St. Michael's Abbey, Farnborough, Hampshire, where he was later joined by his only child, Louis-Napoleon, the Prince Imperial, in 1879, killed in the Zulu War whilst serving in the British army; and by the Empress Eugénie, who enjoyed a remarkably long life, dying in 1920.

Wilhelm I (1797-1888)

Wilhelm Friedrich Ludwig von Hohenzollern, born on 22 March 1797, of the House of Hohenzollern, was King of Prussia from 2 January 1861 and the first German Emperor of a united Germany from 18 January 1871 to his death. Under the leadership of Wilhelm and Otto von Bismarck, as we have seen, Prussia achieved the unification of Germany and the establishment of the German Empire. It has been said that despite his long support of Bismarck as Prime Minister, Wilhelm held strong reservations about some of Bismarck's more reactionary policies, most notably his anti-Catholicism.

Born as a Hohenzollern, militarism was second nature to him; at the age of twelve his father appointed him an officer in the Prussian army, in which he served from 1814 onward. He gained his first battlefield experience when he fought against Napoleon I during the Napoleonic Wars, most notably at Waterloo. He was reportedly a brave soldier, was promoted to captain and won the Iron Cross. The war against France left a lifelong impression on him and he had a long-standing antipathy towards the French.

In 1815 Wilhelm was promoted to major. After 1815 and the defeat of Napoleon, he became a diplomat, engaging in diplomatic missions.

After several subsequent promotions, Wilhelm became a major general, which made him, very conveniently, a spokesman for the Prussian army within the House of Hohenzollern. He argued in favour of a strong, well-trained and well-equipped army. In 1825 he was promoted to commanding general of III Army Corps. In 1840, his older brother, Friedrich Wilhelm IV, became King of Prussia; since he had no children, Wilhelm was first in line to succeed him and thus was given the title Prince of Prussia. During the 'Year of Revolutions' (1848), Wilhelm successfully crushed a revolt in Berlin that aimed to depose the king; however, his extensive use of cannons to suppress demonstrators made him unpopular at the time and earned him the nickname 'Prince Grapeshot'.

His brother, Friedrich Wilhelm IV, suffered a stroke in 1857 and as a result William became Regent, a temporary solution but, when it became clear that the King was not going to recover, the position was made permanent.

Wilhelm I, wearing the regalia of a Freemason.

Friedrich Wilhelm IV.

During his reign he clashed several times with the Prussian parliament about army reforms; Wilhelm and his Minister of War, Albrecht von

Roon, wanted to raise the peacetime army from 150,000 to 200,000 men and boost the annual number of new recruits from 40,000 to 63,000. The most controversial aspect of the plan was to keep the length of military service (already raised in 1856 to two years) at three years. The obvious problem was the matter of paying for this much expanded army; and the differences rose to crisis point in 1862. Wilhelm, eventually got his way, partly by threatening abdication but, far more significantly for the future of Prussia and Germany, appointed Bismarck as Minister President, an approximate equivalent to a British Prime Minister, and Foreign Minister.

Wilhelm was the commander-in-chief of the Prussian forces in the Second Schleswig War against Denmark in 1864 and the Austro-Prussian War in 1866. In 1867 the North German Confederation was created as a federation of the northern and central German state; it was overwhelmingly dominated by Prussia, which provided eighty percent of the population of the Federation. In 1870, during the Franco-Prussian War, Wilhelm was, at least in name, in command of all the German forces at the crucial Battle of Sedan. On 1 February 1870 Wilhelm was proclaimed emperor of a united Germany and, in spite of several attempts to assassinate him, became increasingly popular amongst the people as he grew older. Emperor Wilhelm I died on 9 March 1888 in Berlin after a short illness and was buried on 16 March in the Mausoleum at Park Charlottenburg in Berlin.

Wilhelm I was succeeded by his son, Crown Prince Friedrich, the Crown Prince of Prussia and the German Empire, who became Emperor Friedrich III (although logically he should have been Emperor Friedrich I) and King of Prussia. However, he died of cancer of the throat after just ninety-nine days on the throne. He was succeeded by his oldest son, Wilhelm, who became Kaiser (Emperor) Wilhelm II. Because of the rapid succession of three emperors in one year, 1888 became known as the Year of the Three Emperors.

Mausoleum of Emperor Wilhelm I in Charlottenburg Park, Berlin.

Advice to Tourers and Useful Addresses

The Ardennes region is not very densely populated; it is an area dotted with small villages. The Sedan 1870 battlefields, however, are only a few minutes drive from the cities of Sedan and Stenay. On the former Sedan battlefield, an area of ten by twenty square kilometres, there are only a few places where you can fill up your petrol tank, buy snacks to take with you on your battlefield tour, have a cup of coffee or find a public convenience.

The car tours are all accessible – at least as of the date of publication – in a standard saloon car and in many cases in a small minibus. However, if you are planning a tour in a vehicle that is bigger than a car/campervan, it is advisable to check the route first. Naturally, the car tour stops are all accessible to anyone touring by mountain bike or electric bike.

Petrol/Gas Stations
Balan, Mouzay, Sedan, Stenay

Supermarkets
Balan, Mouzay, Sedan, Stenay

Cafés and/or lunch facilities
Balan, Bazeilles, Daigny, Mouzay, Sedan, Stenay
NOTE: Resteaurants are generally open between 12.00 and 2.00 pm, and from 7.00 pm.

Countryside Code
Please follow the Countryside Code when you are walking in the countryside, and especially when you are crossing over farmland.– leave gates and property as you find them and please take your litter home with you. Do not obstruct farm tracks with your vehicle (or, if you do, stay close by so that you can move it quickly as necessary). It might sound obvious, but do not wander over a field with crops growing in it – there are plenty of excellent spots by the side of roads and tracks that give panoramic views. The roads in the area are generally well maintained – however, they can be narrow, so please walk along them taking due care.

Where to stay
There are numerous B&Bs, hotels and gîtes in the Ardennes. The easiest way to find something to your liking is to look on the internet. Many

B&Bs have a restaurant licence and offer good quality three course meals at reasonable prices. This saves you considerable time on arrival, as you do not have to go out searching for a restaurant; whilst it is also very handy during the rest of your stay.

Ordnance and war relics
Between 1870 and 1945 the area covered in this book saw significant fighting in several wars. Therefore, it is important that you understand some vital realities about this former war zone. It is not a playground and every now and then unthinking tourists, without regard for the consequences, get wounded, or even worse, killed (as happened in the summer of 2018) by engines of war.

The bomb disposal unit in the Meuse and French Ardennes consists of ten men, successors of those who, since the 1920s, day in and day out, put their lives on the line to clear the former battlefields of the deadly heritage of the First and Second World Wars. Every year these men collect some hundred tons of shells of all types – gas, shrapnel or high explosive – as well as hand grenades. Gas shells have the potential to be particularly hazardous; many of these were fired during the 1918 campaigns. Travellers are strongly warned NOT to pick up anything off the ground that looks suspect and to use their common sense. Munitions are designed to kill and sometimes they still do. Remember that rusty metal is an ideal breeding ground for tetanus.

Maps
It is very useful to obtain a general map of the Meuse-Argonne and Ardennes region. If you want to study the area in more detail, the maps in the IGN Série Bleue are highly recommended. The maps you should buy are: Raucourt-et-Flabas, 3010 E, Sedan, 3009 E, Carignan, 3110 O, 3011 SB Vouziers, 3111 SB Stenay. They can be purchased locally (although this is getting harder with every year that passes) or can be ordered from various internet sites. Recent experience shows that the IGN website has become notably easier to use.

Driving in France
In France, motorists drive on the right hand side of the road; all car passengers must wear seat belts. The roads in the Meuse-Argonne area are mostly well maintained. The maximum speed in villages, towns and cities is 50 km/h (although it is increasingly common for sections of road in a built up area to be limited to 30 km/h, particularly near schools), on national roads (N and D roads, i.e. N209, D15) 80 km/h and on motorways 130 km/h unless indicated otherwise (for example, 110 km/h in rain).

Priorité à droite

Give way to traffic coming from your right. If you are driving along a road, anyone joining that road from your right hand side has right of way over you – usually, but not always, indicated by a sign with an 'X'. If you happen to be on a road that has a yellow diamond sign, then anyone on that road has right of way. There are variations, but the wisest course is to assume right of way from the right. Most road intersections have bollards with a red stripe towards the top on the intersecting road(s).

In France, drivers are required by law to carry a <u>yellow luminous vest</u> in the car, in an easily accessible place; should you have a breakdown in France, you *and your passengers* have to wear the highly visible jacket when you get out of your car. Also on the list of items a driver is legally required to carry in his car are a warning triangle, easily accessible in the boot, a first aid kit, a breathalyser – the law is hazy on this but better be safe than sorry – and a sticker for your windscreen that indicates the emissions category of your vehicle. Failure to comply with any of these can result in on the spot fines, usually between €45 and €90.

The weather

In summer it can be very hot in this area. As regards the rest of the year, the weather is usually quite good but from time to time you may need wellington (rubber) boots – though good quality walking boots should suffice, even in winter, and should be a minimum footwear requirement year round. It is always handy to have protective wet weather gear and an umbrella; you never know when you may need them! Tips for a pleasant trip into the forest: put on a well-known brand of insect repellent. Since ticks (carriers of the bacteria that cause Lyme's Disease) are common in forests, it is advisable to cover up when entering these areas i.e. long sleeves and trousers, no matter what time of the year.

Water

It is quite safe to drink tap water in this area. The French continually monitor the quality of drinking water. Some of the walks can be lengthy and so a readily accessible supply of bottled water is advised.

Hospital

Should you be unfortunate enough to require medical aid, there is a hospital in Sedan and the nearby city of Charleville-Mézières. Most doctors and specialists speak English, at least the basics. There are numerous pharmacies and one can usually be found in the bigger towns in the area.

Centre Hospitalier de Sedan
2 avenue Marguerite
08209 SEDAN cedex
+33 (0)3 24 22 80 00

Centre Hospitalier de Charleville Mézières
45 avenue de Manchester
BP 10900
08011 Charleville Mézières cedex
+33 (0)3 24 58 70 70

Guided tours
For guided tours in English or Dutch contact museum19141918@
gmail.com

Acknowledgements

After numerous emails and conversations with Battleground Europe Series editor Nigel Cave, we finally managed to convince Pen & Sword about the importance of covering the Franco-Prussian War battlefields. During this process, Nigel introduced me to P&S author and fellow Franco-Prussian War enthusiast David O'Mara, who is going to write two of the four books planned for the 1870 series.

Another driving force behind this project is my best friend, Bart Metselaar; together we have made many visits to explore the battlefields. Just as in my previous publications for P&S, the excellent maps in the tour section are drawn by Bart. This time he also shared his knowledge about European history with me by taking care of the research for Chapter One. Thanks for your time and effort beyond the call of duty!

Further thanks go to Orla Ryan-Kuiper, for tirelessly proofreading and correcting the manuscript; Monsieur Clement, manager and curator of the outstanding La Dernière Cartouche Museum in Bazeilles, who was always willing to answer my questions, generously shared his knowledge and allowed me to take and use photos from his impressive collection; Didi, my wife, for test walking and driving the tours and for putting up with me ceaselessly nattering on about Napoleon III and 1870. Thanks also go to my brother, Tim, and Nigel Cave, with whom I explored the battlefield on a marvellous summer day on 1 September 2018, exactly 148 years after many of the events described here happened; John and Matthew Cook; Michel Morel, Bas van Dorp and Thibault Mansy, who generously supported me by lending me books, magazines and photographs on the subject. Last, but certainly not least, my thanks to the people at Pen & Sword who put my books together: Matt Jones, Sylvia Menzies, Jon Wilkinson and Dom Allen. It is through their professionalism that you hold this book in your hands.

All errors are solely my responsibility.

Nantillois, February 2020

Selective bibliography and further reading

Some of these books have been out of print for a century or more but are relatively easy to find on line and are very often for sale at a surprisingly low price. I have found Douglas Fermer's relatively recent book (2008), *Sedan 1870*, particularly useful.

1870 L'empire s'ecroule à Sedan, Guy Rey, Jaques Bonfils, Euromedia, Douzy, 2010

Aus meinem Leben, Von Hindenburg, H. Hirzel, Leipzich, Germany, 1920

Atlas de la guerre (1870-71), Amédée Le Faure, Garnier Frères, Paris, France, 1875

Bazeilles 31 août-1er septembre 1870, B. Churlet & J. Cogniet, Imprimerie Félix, Vouziers, France, 2009

Der deutsch-französische krieg 1870-71, *kriegsgeschichtlichen Abteilung des Grossen Generalstabes*, Ernst Siegfried Mittler und Sohn, Belin, Germny, 1874

Die Schlachten von Beaumont und Sedan, Carl Tenera, Oskar Beck Verlachsbuchhandlung, Munchen, Germany, 1893

From Sedan to Saarbruck, By an officer of the Royal Artillery, Helion Books, Solihull, West Midlands, England, 1992

Histoire générale de la guerre franco-allemande (1870-1871), Atlas, Rousset, Jules Tallandier, Paris, France, 1930

Histoire générale de la guerre franco-allemande (1870-1871), Tome 1 & 2, Rousset, Jules Tallandier, Paris, France, 1911

Killed at Saarbruck, Edward Legge, Leonaur, England, 2012

Krieg und Sieg 1970-71, Dr. J. v. Pflugk-Harttung, Verlachsbuchhandlung Alfred Schall, Berllin, Germany, 1896

Sedan 1870, Douglas Fermer, Pen & Sword Books Ltd, Barnsley, England, 2008

Tagesbuch des Deuts-Französischen Krieges 1870/71, Von der Kriegserklärung bis Sedan, Georg Hirth und Julius von Gofen, Alfred Jansfen, Hamburg und Berlin, 1913

The family trees of the kings of France, Jean-Charles Volkmann, Editions Jean-Paul Gisserot, Paris, 2002

The Franco-Prussian War: The German invasion of France 1870-1871, Michael Howard, Routledge, 2001.

The Franco-Prussian War, Geoffrey Wawro, Cambridge University Press, New York, USA, 2010

The reality of war, Léonce Patry, Cassel & Co, London, England, 2001

Zum 25 jährichn Gedächtnis Der Krieg zwischen frankreich und Deutschlands in den Jahren 1870-71, J. Scheibert, Verlach von W. Pauli's, Berlin, Germany, 1895

Index